Len and Sandy Sargent

A Legacy of Activist Philanthropy

By **Robin Tawney Nichols**
with **Scott McMillion**

The University of Montana Press
Missoula, Montana

The University of Montana Press
The University of Montana
32 Campus Drive, Missoula, Montana 59812

Cover photos by Bob Kiesling.
Phil Tawney photo by Mike Meloy.
All photos from the Sargent family collection unless otherwise noted.

Design: Text design, and graphics by Laurie Gigette McGrath
         Marysville, Montana 59640
Cover: Neal Wiegert, UM Printing & Graphic Services
         Laurie Gigette McGrath, Marysville, Montana

The University of Montana Press Committee:
George Dennison - President
Jim Foley – Executive Vice President
Bonnie Allen – Dean of Libraries
Gerald A. Fetz – Dean and Professor Emeritus, College of Arts and Sciences
Harry W. Fritz – Professor/History Department
Rick Graetz – Geography Professor
Keith Graham – Journalism Professor
Ken Price – Director of Printing Services

Printed in the USA by The University of Montana
Printing & Graphic Services, Missoula, Montana
Printed on recycled paper with vegetable-based inks.

Cataloging-in-Publication data is on file at the Library of Congress
ISBN: 978-0-9815760-3-9

 Table of Contents

Preface 1

Introduction 5

Chapter 1: Family Values 9

Chapter 2: Not in Montana's Backyard 25

Chapter 3: The Perfect Conjunction 43

Chapter 4: The Ranch 53

Chapter 5: Two Kinds of Green 69

Chapter 6: Leading From Behind 75

Select Bibliography..89

About the Author..92

Len and Sandy Sargent

 **Preface**

This is the story of Len and Sandy Sargent, an energetic and generous couple who left an indelible mark on Montana and the Greater Yellowstone Ecosystem. It is a story about how two people added their voices and financial support to a growing grassroots movement and helped change the way environmental organizations address state and regional issues.

Politically conservative in an era of social activism, the Sargents retired to their scenic Montana ranch and soon found themselves at odds with their equally conservative neighbors. Where Len and Sandy had sought peace and quiet—away from the urban cacophony of the late-1960s—they discovered a host of threats to the natural resources that had attracted them to their adopted state and region. Many old-time residents either said nothing or welcomed corporate raiders with open arms. The Sargents' choice was simple: Shut up and get along, or speak out and raise a ruckus.

For thinking people, it was a no-brainer. The Sargents abandoned their comfortable retirement and reinvented themselves as activists and philanthropists, dedicating the last third of their lives to protecting wildlife and wild lands.

From the early days of the modern environmental movement, Len and Sandy plunged heart and soul into the fray and gladly contributed their financial resources to a bumper crop of nonprofit organizations. Ultimately, the Sargents established the Cinnabar Foundation to provide financial support, in perpetuity, for conservation advocacy, education, and research in Montana and throughout the area surrounding Yellowstone National Park.

Through the years, Len and Sandy developed deep and lasting relationships with people who shared their passion and commitment. They opened wide their doors and welcomed legions to meetings and retreats at their remote ranch, offering sympathetic ears and soft pillows to a generation of activists.

From the moment I met them, Len and Sandy captured a constant place in my life and heart. At the state capitol in the 1970s, we worked long hours side by side, promoting sound legislation to rein in energy and subdivision development. At the same time, we were building—from the ground up—a year-round organization to monitor the state agencies that dealt with those issues. When my lobbying days abruptly ended with the premature birth of my firstborn, the Sargents brought binoculars to the hospital so visitors could get a good look at him, cocooned in an incubator at the far end of the nursery. With unconditional love and support, Len and Sandy also shared the joy of my girls' births and all the other benchmarks of my family's life. They grieved deeply at the loss of my first husband, whom they loved like a son. And, years later, they embraced my husband-to-be as another member of their extended family.

Sentimental, playful, and practical gifts from the Sargents grace the walls and drawers of our home. Among them: books, games, and puzzles with conservation themes; cassette tapes and compact discs of music recorded by their favorite artists and friends; a dozen no-iron cloth napkins in a rainbow of colors for easy entertaining; a scooped rubber tool that Sandy swore she—and, therefore, I—could not bake without. I wore out the latter and promptly replaced it, not because of its usefulness but because "Sandy's spatula" reminds me of Sandy.

Through their personal gifts, the Sargents taught me to always pay attention to the needs and interests of others. Sandy did not wait for a birthday or holiday when she discovered that I suffered from the chronic pain of carpal tunnel syndrome. To help me continue my passion for baking, she sent me a battery-operated flour sifter to substitute for my mechanical version.

Len was the first to stay in the guest "suite" of our new home. When he departed, he left a housewarming gift of bathroom accessories and a polite note suggesting that we replace the single bed with a king-sized one. Our space was too modest for a king but thanks to Len's thoughtful suggestion, we soon replaced our guest single with a queen-sized bed. Presumably, our next overnight visitors slept better than Len!

Toward the end of the Sargents' lives, I was privileged to return a bit of the kindness that they had shown my family for so many years. My help was not much, compared to theirs, yet I'd like to think I lightened their load a bit by providing companionship, running errands, and storing the "extras" between their visits to Missoula for medical care. Now that Len and Sandy are gone, I'd like to think I am helping them still by serving on the board of the Cinnabar Foundation and by chronicling their lives on these pages.

The Sargents' biography project began in 1995 after Sandy received a chilling diagnosis of myleodysplastic syndrome—a pre-leukemia—within months of my husband's own death from the same brand of leukemia that ultimately would claim her life as well. Numbering only four people at the time, the Cinnabar board faced a hard reality: Its membership already had dropped by a quarter with the loss of Phil Tawney and, even if Sandy regained her health, the Sargents were aging. The story about how the Sargents wove activism with philanthropy was worth telling but would be forgotten over time unless someone preserved it. Thus, the Cinnabar Foundation board decided to publish this joint biography to introduce Len and Sandy to the staffs and boards of the nonprofit groups we fund; to the individuals who receive fellowships, awards, and staff positions in their names; and to other interested parties.

To this end, our narrative celebrates the lives of two people who were not content to stand on the sidelines and "let George do it" and hopefully will inspire others—of lesser or greater means—to also be generous with their time and financial resources for the good of wildlife, wild lands, and community.

Giving voice to the Sargents' story are Len and Sandy themselves in decades of personal correspondence; in a videotaped interview by Gayle Joslin; in notes from interviews by me; and in a formal recorded interview by Susan Neel, commissioned by the Cinnabar Foundation. Scott McMillion added depth to the Sargents' portrait by taking down the stories of many of their friends and colleagues, including Gordon Brittan, Bill Bryan, Barnaby Conrad, Susan Cottingham, Jim Jensen, Bob Kiesling, Sanna Porte, Jim Posewitz, Tom Roy, Rick Hubbard Sargent, Judi Stauffer, Ernest Turner, Pat Williams, and me.

Scott produced an important first draft, which he graciously passed on to me for editing. As a close friend of the Sargents who had shared their lives and their soapbox, I could not avoid my own flood of memories as I read Scott's manuscript, and I added to his work in such a way that it became my own. To Scott, I apologize for the takeover, but know that I owe you my unending thanks. Thank you, as well, to all those mentioned above and to the Sargents' daughter Kerri Hubbard Hart; my husband William Nichols; my parents, Bob and Cidney Brown; Kay Ellerhoff; John Hurley; Ellen Knight; and Kathy Thomas. Clearly, any errors in the text are my full responsibility.

Because much of what follows amounts to shared, or at least similar, experiences by those interviewed, I have erred on the side of omitting attribution as much as possible. Direct quotes and paraphrased remembrances appear only when they yield unique observations or clarification.

To those welcomed by Len's warm chuckle or waylaid by Sandy's conspiratorial confidences, please forgive me as I seize the writer's prerogative and occasionally interject my own Sargent memories to the telling of their story. I realize that some of your reflections may overlap with mine; if so, substitute your name when you read the first person. Everyone who knew Len and Sandy rightfully savors special memories and I urge all to share them with each other, with your families, and with your organizations. By the telling, the Sargents' story will continue to affect the landscape and people of Montana and the Greater Yellowstone Ecosystem.

Len and Sandy Sargent were ordinary people who left an extraordinary legacy.

There is a lesson here for all of us.

Robin Tawney Nichols
Missoula, Montana
Spring 2008

 **Introduction**

A dozen horses cut loose from the forest edge and sped across the high mountain meadow, not as the crow flies, but in a broad slalom through the lush summer grass. With their wide-set eyes and serpentine path, the herd could easily follow the progress of an ancient gelding, some distance behind but carefully picking his way toward them. When the younger horses sensed they had ranged too far, they abruptly halted and dropped their noses to the earth, lipping the plentiful grass. In time, old Zeke ambled up. The herd nuzzled their hellos and then patiently resumed grazing, respecting their wizened leader's need to rest before he sent them off on a new course.

Leonard and Sandy Sargent owned Zeke and the rest of the herd. While they seldom rode, they enjoyed watching how their horses moved as one through the expansive pastures of their Montana ranch, just below the northern rim of Yellowstone National Park. Len bought the first horses for this remuda in the early 1960s, and he knew all there was to know about each one. Both he and Sandy marveled at how, long ago, the herd had selected a rather unremarkable horse as its leader.

Len especially liked Zeke and he knew the younger horses did, too, because they never nipped or kicked him, even though Zeke was the oldest and weakest member of the herd. The other horses seemed to know that this pot-bellied gelding, neither strong nor athletic even in his prime, was especially wise and they quite naturally deferred to his instinct and sense of manners. A bit bemused by this equine pecking order, Len would give voice to his observation: "Zeke is still a leader, but he leads from behind now."

Len and Sandy were more than a little wistful whenever they shared their memories of the old gelding leading from behind as the herd traversed the wide-open spaces of Cinnabar Basin. By the time they told their stories in the mid-1990s, Zeke had passed on and the Sargents had sold their beloved ranch and moved to town. As the years caught up to them, Len and Sandy had never considered how much they were like their old favorite, leading others from behind, but when a visitor pointed out the obvious, they understood immediately.

"I like that," said Len, pulling Sandy closer to his side. "When you can lead from the rear, you've got it made. I'd be very proud to follow in old Zeke's footsteps."

Leading from behind came naturally to Len and Sandy.

Earlier in their lives, they had chosen to lead young people—Len as a teacher and coach, Sandy as a parent and personal assistant at a church and a private day school. Then in the turbulent 1960s, leading others became difficult as youthful protests and outright disrespect abraded their conservative souls.

So, the Sargents retired, seeking solitude and unending peace at their isolated ranch, embraced by a circle of high mountain peaks that offered, to their delight, a boundless parade of megafauna. Their tranquility, however, was short-lived, irreparably broken when they discovered that the very wildness they treasured also attracted the attention of dam builders, resource developers, off-road vehicle users, and New Age settlers. All were poised to exploit the Sargents' adopted state and the area surrounding nearby Yellowstone National Park.

Having witnessed the devastation wrought by unchecked development in other parts of the country, the Sargents were compelled to leave their tender sanctuary and speak out. They joined a small, but dedicated, corps of activists—mostly young and many a little scruffy. Over the next 25 years, the corps grew in number and, with the Sargents' help, built strong organizations that fought consistently, though not always successfully, for sound natural resource policies at every level of government.

Len and Sandy worked in simple and direct ways, writing letters, disseminating information, attending hearings and meetings, lobbying the state legislature and Congress, rallying others to protect the environment they had come to love. The Sargents never shrank from a tough fight, but they decried the hostility and bitterness so often a part of environmental debates and always tried to conduct themselves with humor and humility. In doing so, they taught a generation of young activists the meaning of tenacity, good manners, grace under pressure, and how to hold their ground.

The long perspective of their lives had taught Len and Sandy about the limitations of crisis thinking. Although they often worked within the exigency of modern environmentalism—rushing, as Sandy said, "from one end of the state to the other"—the Sargents appreciated the need to sustain organizations for the long haul, and they generously supported those groups with cold, hard cash. They discovered they could double their effectiveness by blending activism and philanthropy, and that potent combination became their signature.

Within the birthing stories of many long-lived environmental groups in this region are tales of how, by their timely counsel, activism, and financial contributions, the Sargents made a fundamental difference in the way natural resource issues were addressed. For 30 years, all across Montana and, especially, in their larger neighborhood around Yellowstone Park, they set new standards for unwavering commitment, hard work, and generosity. By their unassuming example, Len and Sandy paved the way for others to contribute their own wealth, experience, and expertise.

The legacy of the Sargents' activist philanthropy lives on in the Cinnabar Foundation, a charitable vehicle they created in 1983 to help perpetuate, as Len wrote on the foundation's tenth anniversary, "rivers running clear and free, mountains shouldering deep forests, and wolves racing through the shadows of the January moon."

The Sargents helped build the herd and then, like old Zeke, they led from behind.

The Packard girls: Debby, Sandy holding Sabra, and Karen, 1931.

Len and his parents in Coronado, California, undated.

CHAPTER 1
Family Values

L en Sargent must have used the same line a million times, repeating it whenever someone asked why he and Sandy married in mid-life despite meeting some 30 years earlier: "I wanted to wait and see how she turned out," he would say, and then he would give his diminutive wife a squeeze.

The Sargent love story began in 1939 at an afternoon tea dance hosted by The Taft School, the all-boys' school in Watertown, Connecticut. As one of Taft's youngest faculty members, Len was assigned to chaperone this particular dance, and it was there that he spotted Sandy, a vivacious 17-year-old senior from Westover School on the arm of a boy her own age. Many years later, Sandy would report that the handsome bachelor teacher was "wolfing his students' dates," a claim Len could not deny because he was so obviously smitten by a certain young woman.

With due propriety, Len shelved his ardor until Sandy graduated from high school, whereupon she complicated dating logistics by leaving Westover and Middlebury, Connecticut, to return to her home in Bronxville, New York. Separated by distance, Sandy and Len dated only a few times that summer. Fall came and the couple put their budding romance on hold as Sandy moved south to Virginia and Sweet Briar College, and Len resumed his teaching and coaching duties at The Taft School. Barely two years later, as the United States prepared to join the Allies in World War II, Len and Sandy separated indefinitely, not unlike so many other young couples of their era.

Years became decades, yet they managed to keep in touch, mostly through mutual friends, holiday cards, and an occasional visit. Their infrequent contact, however, proved sufficient. By the 1960s, the spark kindled in their youth ignited, and in 1969, Len and Sandy married and moved to Montana. Together at last, they embarked on new careers as ranchers and conservation leaders.

By then, Leonard Rundlett Sargent Jr. was 56. Merriam Sands "Sandy" Packard Hubbard was 47.

Leonard

Born in Baltimore, Maryland, on December 30, 1912, Len was the only child of Gladys Grandy and Commander Leonard Rundlett Sargent. As a 3-year-old, Len moved with his family to the Panama Canal Zone, where his father took command of the recently completed locks and 50-mile waterway linking the Atlantic and Pacific oceans.

As the United States debated its subsequent entry into World War I, Leonard Sr. faced an unprecedented challenge to design the military management of this vital and vulnerable engineering marvel. Nothing Leonard Sr. had learned at the U.S. Naval Academy or in his subsequent duty assignments had prepared him for this job. Nevertheless, he proceeded undaunted and, by his leadership, set high standards for those who later took up his post in the Canal Zone.

Commander Sargent's can-do attitude also rubbed off on his only child, who later spoke reverently of his father and marveled at how the Panamanians had even named a street in his honor, a fact confirmed by a faded photograph. (Alas, on two pilgrimages to the Canal Zone in the 1990s, Leonard Jr. and Sandy failed to find Leonard R. Sargent Street.)

Leonard Jr.'s few memories of the three years his family spent in Panama were shaped by the privileges, responsibilities, and status befitting his father's rank, which included hosting the Prince of Wales in the posh Sargent quarters next door to the residence of the Canal Zone's governor. More importantly, Len began to absorb lessons that became persistent life themes and echoed the military values exemplified by his father: respect, integrity, honor, duty, and loyalty.

As Len grew to manhood, these classic and fundamental tenets, as well as citizenship and social responsibility, were reinforced by the all-male boarding schools he attended—Webb School in Coronado, California, and The Gunnery in Washington, Connecticut—and by frequent visits to his parents' ever-changing homes at his father's ports of call.

After graduating from Princeton University in 1937 with a degree in geology and teaching briefly at The Taft School, Len responded to his generation's challenges in Europe and the Pacific and, like his father, enlisted in the Navy. As an educator, but with no other qualification, Ensign, then Lieutenant Junior Grade, Leonard Sargent Jr. found himself teaching navigation at Columbia University in New York City and at the University of Washington in Seattle. Like his father mastering the "how-to" of his Panama Canal assignment, Len quickly mastered Navy navigation.

Sandy

While Len's early years kept him on the go, bouncing between prep schools and his itinerant Navy parents, Sandy's life revolved around her large extended family and friends in the affluent suburb of Bronxville, just north of Manhattan's Upper Eastside.

Born in Bronxville on October 13, 1921, Merriam Sands "Sandy" Packard was the eldest child of Sabra Beaumont and William Guthrie Packard. Sandy's father published law books, including a classic and essential tool for legal research, *Shepard's Citations.* Sandy's mother tended the Packard home and taught her four young daughters to be proper, well-rounded gentlewomen.

Easterners drawn to the West by the novelty of ranch life, Sabra and William Packard met at an Arizona dude ranch and honeymooned in Yellowstone Park. In 1922, the couple began a summer tradition as the first of four guests at Elkhorn Ranch in Montana's Gallatin Canyon. Sabra and William retreated annually to the remote dude ranch and later introduced their daughters to its relaxed hospitality and spectacular setting. As each reached the magic age of 12 and learned to ride horseback, Sandy, Debby, Karen, and young Sabra joined their parents for a cross-country train trip and a heavenly month of Old West adventures, just a mile from Yellowstone's northwest corner.

With riding lessons and summers at Elkhorn Ranch, the Packard girls became proficient horsewomen. Sandy, especially, enjoyed competing and exhibited grace under pressure in 1933 by winning a blue ribbon at the prestigious Good Hands National Horse Show in New York City's Madison Square Garden. Despite her success in the show ring, Sandy, like her sisters, abruptly ended her riding career at age 16, because her mother had determined that, after 16, show riding was no longer a suitable activity for proper young women. Sandy respected her mother's dictum, saying that, as a teenager, she had plenty of other interests.

The discipline Sandy learned through competitive riding, coupled with the freedom of her summers in Montana, complemented her lessons at the all-girls' Westover School, which challenged its teen-age students to think independently and to grow intellectually and spiritually. Westover also stressed integrity, responsibility, and commitment to community—basic values that became Sandy's life themes and echoed those of Leonard.

In 1939, war was stirring in Europe as Sandy graduated from Westover and enrolled in Sweet Briar College. Two years later, pulled by patriotism and duty, she left her liberal arts studies to attend a yearlong secretarial program at the Katharine Gibbs School in New York City. With the United

States fully engaged in World War II, Sandy easily found employment as a civilian secretary for the Counter Intelligence Corps and later for the Aerial Port of Embarkation at LaGuardia Airport. In the latter assignment, she processed VIP travelers and "people who had to go in a hurry," including numerous actors and actresses. Overall, she later recalled, her wartime jobs were "quite fun" and "very interesting," as well as a way to be of service to her nation.

Life on the Packard home front also was changing. In 1941, Sandy's parents divorced after a lengthy separation, and Sandy began dating a hometown boy, Thomas Bassett Hubbard, who soon enlisted in the Army

Sandy, the accomplished equestrian, undated.

Air Forces Reserve. Sandy and Tom married a year later when Sandy completed her studies at Katharine Gibbs, but they saw little of each other for the duration of the war. While the new Mrs. Hubbard worked for the government in New York City, Lt. Hubbard flew treacherous routes "over the hump" in Burma.

Winter God

Meanwhile, Len's new navigation skills led to assignments in antisubmarine warfare and convoy protection aboard vessels crossing the Atlantic, chasing Nazi submarines in the Mediterranean, and creating a strategic diversion to distract German forces from the real action in Normandy on D-Day. At war's end, after five years of Navy service and another well-earned promotion, Commander Leonard R. Sargent chose to return to The Taft School, teaching science and mathematics while coaching hockey and tennis.

With Sandy married to Tom Hubbard, Len resumed his bachelor life. He lived in an apartment on the fourth floor of Taft's gothic red brick dormitory, surrounded by his students and dining every day with a dozen of them in a formal rotation that encouraged interaction between the boys and their teachers.

Whether in class, in the dining room, or on the playing field, Len modeled character, taught fair play, and nurtured courage. In Len's book, sportsmanship was supremely important, so he prepared his teams to accept winning graciously, to cope with losing, and to appreciate the value of persisting. His hockey team dubbed him the "Winter God."

To help his players do their best, Len made sure they practiced on a good rink. In 1949, frustrated by New England's freeze-thaw winters and iffy pond ice, the determined coach—with the blessing of the Taft administration—single-handedly raised nearly $250,000 to build the first artificial hockey rink of any prep school in the region. Ever the teacher, Len marshaled his students to lay the pipes for the rink, foreshadowing the role of foreman he would later assume at his Montana ranch.

In 1956, Len once again upped his team's advantage and confirmed his ability as a fundraiser by convincing the Weyerhaeuser family to make a sizable donation to enclose the Taft rink. Now Len's hockey team could skate year-round. (Forty-odd years later, the retired coach continued to promote hockey by raising money for an artificial ice rink in Bozeman, Montana.)

As Taft's coach, Len cut a distinctive figure with his tam and ever-present pipe, prompting those at rival private prep schools to assume he was

The Winter God coached to win but stressed sportsmanship above all, undated. *The Taft School.*

Chevy, a fixture in Len's classroom, undated. *The Taft School.*

pompous and overbearing. However, Taft students worshipped him and Len's support for his team was total. His reserved leadership made it possible for The Taft School to compete successfully both nationally and internationally. Much to the chagrin of other prep schools, Len's teams totally dominated ice hockey in western New England from 1951 to 1969, the year he retired. Under Coach Sargent's guidance, the Taft teams won championship after championship and never finished less than second.

Winter God, indeed.

The road traveled

While Len enjoyed a comfortable and predictable life at Taft, punctuated by the thrill of athletic contests, Sandy faced a series of challenges. At the end of World War II, her father married his secretary and moved west to start a new life and a new family in Colorado Springs, Colorado. Meanwhile, Sandy and Tom Hubbard settled in Bronxville, then in Rye, New York, where Tom became an advertising executive and Sandy busied herself as a consummate suburban homemaker and mother of two children adopted at birth: Rick in 1952 and Kerri in 1954.

By 1957, the Hubbards' "picture-perfect" marriage had come apart at the seams, and Sandy and Tom divorced. Returning to Bronxville, where her mother still resided, Sandy supported her children as secretary to the organist and choir director of the Dutch Reformed Church. Through the late 1950s and 1960s, she stayed busy and focused, dividing her time and considerable energies between her kids and her job, always buttressed by the love and support of her mother, sisters, and cousins. Her new role as a single working mother ran counter to the "Ozzie and Harriet" norm and raised a few eyebrows among the Colonial Dames and members of the Riverside Country Club, where she kept up with old friends. At a Junior League concert in Greenwich, Connecticut, she briefly renewed one friendship—with Leonard R. Sargent.

By 1961, Sandy was ready to leave her hometown so she queried her large network of family and friends. Rick's godfather, Edward Talmadge, a Denver real estate businessman, found her a job as assistant to the headmaster of the Denver Country Day School. Sandy jumped at the opportunity and moved her little family west that year, shortly before Len bought a ranch to the north.

Backing into ranching

Len enjoyed being around young people and he loved the West. Every summer while teaching at Taft, he headed toward the Rocky Mountains, usually bringing along a carload of students to share his adventures. For most of those years, the bachelor teacher towed a bulky Airstream trailer on

Rick, Kerri, and Sandy Hubbard, Bronxville, New York, 1960 or 1961.

Taft work crew, 1966.

Len Sargent, breakfast chef.

a sweeping search for a cabin or 20 to 40 acres of bare land along the spine of the western states. As he looked for that ideal spot, Len and his lucky companions explored basins and valleys from New Mexico to Alaska, setting up extensive base camps, and hiking and fishing in the wild country they found.

In 1962, after wandering the West for more than 15 summers, Len found his home in Montana's Cinnabar Basin, a wild and stunning, mountain-rimmed bowl just north of Yellowstone National Park. Only a handful of rugged cattle ranchers shared the remote basin with grizzly bears, wolverines, elk, and bighorn sheep. The proximity to Yellowstone also offered Len a spiritual link with his distant relative, Nathaniel P. Langford. Nearly a century earlier, Langford had played a key role in establishing the world's first national park and served as Yellowstone's first superintendent.

With a small inheritance and savings he had tucked away by living in the Taft dorm, Len had searched for a cabin and a little acreage in the mountains, but in Cinnabar Basin, he hit the jackpot. "Conditions were such that I ended up with a small ranch," he later related matter of factly, as if his purchase was meant to be. Len bought 2,000 acres from rancher Jack McDonald, a combination of open pastures and timbered mountain faces at the end of a 10-mile-long steep and winding, mostly one-lane rutted road that began in Corwin Springs, a tiny outpost along the Yellowstone River.

The hollowed-out bowl cradling Len's new ranch had been created eons earlier by moving rivers of ice as they slowly ground away the sides of the 10,000-foot mountains of the Gallatin Range. From that high country now tumbled a multitude of streams overflowing with snowmelt to nourish the fine, lush grass of Cinnabar Basin. Good cow country in the summer, the glaciated valley became an icebox throughout the long and bitter winter. Len knew this seasonal harshness had discouraged development and helped to keep the basin wild. In a moderate climate, land this close to a national park would have been carved up long ago for recreational development and second homes.

As Len took stock of his new property, he could barely see evidence of man's labors beyond barbed wire fences, a few log buildings, and a smattering of bad roads. So, the prep school teacher rolled up his sleeves and quickly learned the essentials of land ownership in the rural West: "I discovered that with the ranch went water rights, and if you didn't use them, you'd lose them. And with the ranch went grazing permits, and if you didn't use those, not only would you lose [them], but also somebody else would have their cattle going through your broken fences. So, I decided I'd better start ranching. I think that's called 'backing into ranching.' I enjoyed it thoroughly."

Before long, Len doubled his acreage, buying an adjacent spread from a struggling rancher. By his purchase, Len put an end to Kaspar Friedly's money woes and kept him on year-round as foreman. "Kap was able to continue what he had been doing in twice the space," recalled Sandy. "And not have to pay for it," Len added. "That's the ideal ranch."

Having found his "best spot," Len retired the lumbering Airstream trailer. Summers away from The Taft School took on a new focus as, each year, Len rounded up a new clutch of students and headed for the newly christened Sargent Ranch.

The prep school ranch hands spent long days stacking hay bales, mending fences, and chopping wood to heat the cabin, but they also were allowed plenty of free time to swim in the ranch ponds, catch the pure strain of Yellowstone cutthroat trout in icy creeks, and hike ridgelines that offered a spectacular view of Yellowstone Park.

The Sargent Ranch became an idyllic summer haven, so much so that, in some years, an unwieldy number of Taft boys clamored to come west, forcing Len to assign them to shifts of several weeks each. Throughout the 1960s, the ranch exuded a manly atmosphere, with assigned chores and plenty of snoring in the bunkhouse.

Love revisited

Meanwhile, Sandy embraced her new life, joining the Junior League of Denver and luring her eastern relatives to the Rockies for fun-filled ski vacations. Edward Talmadge, Rick's godfather and a keen businessman, sensed the coming ski boom at Vail, Colorado, and urged Sandy to buy property there. She heeded Talmadge's advice and built a little A-frame chalet, thus outfoxing the stampede of glitterati that soon followed. Sandy always chuckled that the wealthy newcomers built their expensive retreats beneath the cliffs, while her modest mountain cottage was "on the sunny side of the street."

Since Sandy loved to drive, summers would find her and her kids on the road, often making transcontinental trips to visit relatives. Other times, their summer adventures were closer to home. In 1967, fondly remembering her own childhood summers at Elkhorn Ranch, Sandy drove Rick and Kerri north to Yellowstone National Park and made a memorable detour to the Sargent Ranch.

The ranch and its owner made an immediate impression on Rick, who was then 15 years old. "I was wide-eyed," Rick later remembered. "There were horses to ride and for a kid at that age, it was very exciting, adventurous, and beautiful. Back in those days, the road was very primitive going up into Cinnabar Basin, just dirt tracks the last couple miles going into the ranch."

Back in Denver, Rick and Kerri never suspected how that fun-filled visit added fuel to the fire between Len and their mother. Though Len and Sandy seldom saw each other over the years, "we pretty much knew where the other one was through mutual friends and all that," Sandy recalled. When Len came to Colorado Springs for a hockey tournament, he phoned Sandy, and "we started all over again," she remembered. The old spark had become a flame, and when love finally blooms, it is a powerful and consuming thing.

In the spring of 1969, following a romantic getaway in Vail, Sandy traveled to Bronxville to visit her mother. She returned with a surprise for her teenagers.

"I remember my mother sitting us down in the living room and saying, 'Well, kids, what would you think if I got married?' " Rick recalled, still marveling at the seeming suddenness. "It was kind of a shock to Kerri and myself, but what are you going to say at that age? A couple years after that first visit (with Len at his ranch), she was asking what we thought about her marrying this guy. A couple months later, they got married in June.

"My life got turned around."

Blending lives

Big changes also were in store for the Winter God. After 30 years of teaching and coaching, culminating in Taft's greatest hockey season ever, Len abruptly retired. On June 13, 1969, the confirmed bachelor married Sandy Packard Hubbard, and immediately took up full-time residence in Cinnabar Basin. Literally overnight, the manly ranch became home to a family of four.

For Len, the move signaled a clean break from his frustration and disappointment in teaching and coaching during the Vietnam era. He was sick and tired of what he saw as fickleness and lack of commitment on the part of his students and players. Their "do-your-own-thing" attitudes collided headlong with the honor, respect for authority, and good-citizen values Len had exemplified throughout his life. Fed up, Len left Taft, married for the first time, and moved west. In the bargain, he acquired an angry stepson and an equally rebellious stepdaughter, neither of whom wanted to leave the life and friends they had in Denver for life at the end of the road.

For Sandy, the move to the Sargent Ranch promised a comfortable fit, a reminder of her carefree adolescent summers at Elkhorn Ranch. Even the terrain was familiar since both ranches lay near the northwest boundary of Yellowstone Park, just on opposite sides of the Gallatin Range. But, in

The blended family: Rick, Sandy, Len, and Kerri, 1969.

truth, the transition to the ranch wasn't easy for anyone in the newly blended family.

Choosing not to enroll Rick and Kerri in Gardiner's tiny high school—a harrowing commute from the ranch over treacherous roads, no matter what the season—Sandy and Len followed family tradition and sent them to boarding schools. For Rick, school now meant Fountain Valley School in Colorado Springs, near Sandy's father, and for Kerri, St. Mary's in the Mountains School in Littleton, New Hampshire, where Sandy's sister Debby McIlwaine and her family lived. Debby taught English at St. Mary's and her husband John served the prep school as headmaster.

At ages 17 and nearly 15, Rick and Kerri both felt uprooted. Through a decision they never made, they were forced to leave lifelong friends and the security and familiarity of their urban home for new schools and a new life—summers and holidays—in the truly Wild West.

To make matters worse, the strong bond between Sandy and her children, forged over the dozen years since her divorce, seemed stretched to its limits as Rick and Kerri now shared their mother with a stepfather. As the only child of an upwardly mobile Navy officer, Len had attended boarding schools and had lived away from his family for most of his life. A splendid teacher and coach of other people's children, Len knew next to nothing about family relationships. Furthermore, his previous home had been a Taft dormitory and, before that, Navy barracks—both hierarchical settings and hardly homey.

With their mother's remarriage, Rick and Kerri came home from their boarding schools and later colleges to "Camp Sargent," drawing summer-long duty as overseers of the annual influx of up to 15 preppy ranch hands. Predictably, Rick and Kerri rebelled some, and Sandy tried hard to mediate and juggle her attentions between her children and her new husband.

Nesting

During their first year as a married couple, Len and Sandy retreated to Denver as soon as icy winds blasted their drafty homestead cabin. By their second year, the Sargents had winterized the old building and added a furnace. The first of several additions and remodeling projects soon expanded the cabin's footprint, engulfing the original log home and including large bedrooms and baths for Rick and Kerri. A massive master suite on the home's new second floor boasted the largest imaginable walk-in closet, chock-full of high-end women's clothing in Sandy's favorite color combination of royal blue and spring green.

Sandy poured herself into decorating, directing workers to whitewash pine paneling and to paint and paper other walls in her signature hues. Her colors dominated every surface of the home's interior—its carpets, fixtures, and furnishings. Over the years, artwork filled nearly every inch of wall space; a portrait of Len's father, in his admiral's uniform, always commanded attention over the living room hearth.

Other building additions and upgrades included creature comforts like a solar-heated outdoor swimming pool (once a terrifying plunge for a young moose), sauna, and Jacuzzi. Yet the Sargents' home remained cozy, comfortable, and unassuming—always a welcoming place to live and work, entertain, and celebrate the wild country surrounding the ranch and beyond.

On summer nights during the early years on the Sargent Ranch, as many as 10 people crowded around the dining room table: Len, Sandy, Rick, Kerri, and any of the constant stream of adult guests who happened to be there at the time. At a second table on the enclosed porch sat the perennial gang of student ranch hands, including a second generation of Taft students, some following the footsteps of fathers who had scouted the West with Len many years before. Coeds joined the Tafties, in deference to Sandy and Kerri Hubbard, who invited teens from other prep schools, as well as the children of Sandy's friends and friends of friends.

Dinnertime topped off the young ranch hands' long, hard days, which they spent helping Len and Kap, and then Kap's successor Al Jensen, as they made improvements and went about the chores of a working cattle ranch. The teens learned to cook at Sandy's side as she prepared endless meals for the hungry crew, and threw balls for her eager black Labrador retriever. A few of them also helped Sandy nurse tender plants in a greenhouse built onto the side of an outbuilding and scratch at the high elevation soils until flowers bloomed.

Love bloomed as well, and not just for Len and Sandy. One summer, the ranch crew included Walter "Trip" Hart, who later became Kerri's husband and father to Sandy and Len's three granddaughters, Calley, Grace, and Taylor. Son Rick brought home his college sweetheart and future wife, Judi Stauffer, and together they found joy in each other and in the mountains surrounding Cinnabar Basin.

Annual holiday letters, written in Sandy's breathless prose, shared news of these weddings and the grandchildren and grand-dogs that followed, as well as visits by family and friends; updates on ranch life and travels; reunions; and, of course, reports on Sandy's labs, Len's golden retrievers, and Zeke, the old saddle horse. Highlights of unusual wildlife sitings, while sometimes hilarious, always included lessons in ecology, like this one:

> A meager white pine nut crop and green fall brought down the bears galore in much of Montana—both black and grizzly—even one sitting in our incinerator sorting thru it only hours after a burning—one warm butt! It was a fascinating time—tho' the dogs weren't too happy!

As the Sargents became engaged in the debates over environmental issues facing their adopted state and region, updates on their advocacy filled at least one-third of the single-spaced, typed letter. Always squeezed into the margin was a personal hand-written note from either Len or Sandy.

Eventually, the detritus that drove Len to retreat from teaching and coaching invaded the remote sanctuary of the Sargent Ranch, and recreational drugs began to accompany the summer crews.

"It was great until drugs came onto the scene, and then I just said, 'No,' " Sandy said years later. "I'm not going to cope with it with other people's children. It's enough to do my own."

"Looking back on it, we were taking a big risk," Len reflected. "It's very risky to have youngsters running tractors and all that kind of stuff. And the thought of having a youngster riding a tractor who might also be bombed on drugs was more than we were willing to cope with."

The number of preppy ranch hands diminished anyway as Rick and Kerri got older and Len's separation from Taft grew. By the mid-1970s, only a handful of teens joined Rick, Kerri, Judi, and Trip for summers at the

Sandy and Len reunited, 1969.

"Camp Sargent" with Rick Hubbard, far right, 1969.

ranch. By the late-1970s, the Sargents purchased a mechanized bale-stacker, allowing the foreman and one helper to do the work of 15 teens. Negating the need for extra help, the new equipment signaled the end of "Camp Sargent" and the beginning of true family life, according to Judi Stauffer. The Hubbard-Sargents now supped as a family: Rick on Sandy's right and Kerri on Len's right. As tensions eased, Sandy's children began to appreciate the freedom of living in and coming home to a wild and magnificent setting. Gradually, the individuals comprising the household at the Sargent Ranch drew closer and, at last, Len became a father figure to Sandy's children. A few years after the death of Tom Hubbard, when Rick and Kerri were well into their thirties, Len formally adopted them.

In 1992, Rick and his wife Judi honored his parents by establishing the Leonard and Sandy Sargent Graduate Fellowship in Environmental Studies at The University of Montana, helping to ensure that future generations of environmental activists would continue the work that had become his parents' passion.

After Len passed on in 1997, Rick honored him twice more by adding Sargent to his surname and by assuming Len's seat on the board of the Cinnabar Foundation.

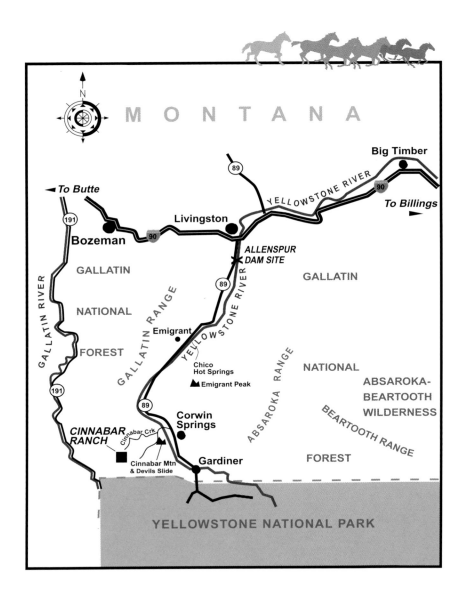

CHAPTER 2
Not in Montana's Backyard

A thing is right when it tends to preserve the integrity,
stability, and beauty of the biotic community.
It is wrong when it tends otherwise. – Aldo Leopold

Rich with an abundance of natural resources, the Sargents' adopted state had a long history of pillage by outsiders—national and multinational corporations that gouged, scraped, and cut, then took their profits out of state and never looked back. While extractive industries brought people and jobs to Montana, they created inevitable cycles of boom and bust, leaving the state with a scarred land and a wary people, without the means to reclaim damaged landscapes or to support jobless workers and their families.

A new round of challenges faced Montana just as the Sargents moved, lock, stock, and teenagers to Cinnabar Basin. This time around, the corporate raiders proclaimed that the good citizens of the Northern Plains—especially Montanans—were honor-bound to share their hefty cache of energy resources with the rest of the nation, even if it meant sacrificing their clean skies and pure water.

In the late 1960s and early 1970s, the world's most powerful country was in a dither over predictions of impending energy shortages. Then, as now, dependence on foreign oil fueled the frenzy. The first energy crisis reached its apex in 1973 with an embargo on oil controlled by the Organization of Petroleum Export Countries (OPEC), a coalition of nations in the Middle East. Then, as now, many in the United States sought full-scale development of our domestic resources to prevent blackouts and brownouts throughout the nation, but especially in our largest cities. Energy conservation and alternative fuel sources received only lip service.

Replacing foreign oil with high-sulfur coal from the eastern United

States was out of the question. While that coal had been a traditional energy source, when burned to produce electricity, it released toxic byproducts in amounts that far exceeded pollution standards for densely populated areas set by the 1970 National Clean Air Act.

Thus, the nation turned to the clear skies and the distant coalfields of the Yellowstone River drainage. Overlapping the sparsely populated states of Montana, Wyoming, and North Dakota, the Fort Union Formation boasted as many as 1.5 trillion tons of low-sulfur coal, less polluting than its high-sulfur eastern cousin. Much of the western coal could easily be strip-mined since it lay just 10 to 100 feet beneath the surface in beds up to 120 feet thick. Montana alone harbored nearly one-fourth of the nation's recoverable coal, including 57 percent of its low-sulfur reserve, virtually undisturbed. Montana's mother lode had been barely dented by the little bit of mining that occurred from 1912 to the 1940s to provide fuel for the locomotives of the Northern Pacific Railway; that activity ceased when diesel engines replaced the coal burners.

All was quiet in the coalfields until the early 1970s, when new air pollution regulations and the politics of foreign oil spurred a black gold rush.

Boiler room of the nation

Facing the country's first "energy crisis," America targeted Montana as "the boiler room of the nation," and many Montanans took offense. They had had enough of the state's historic boom and bust cycles and were determined to allow development only on Montana's terms.

Bolstering this bid for self-determination were more than 20 years of vigilance and thoughtful due diligence by concerned citizens and the state Fish and Game Department (now Department of Fish, Wildlife & Parks). In mid-century, a series of progressive department directors had forecast growing threats to all the state's natural resources and had positioned the agency as a key player in determining their fate. Water use was at the top of the list, and it was a good thing because all-out development of the windswept coalfields would require massive amounts of water in a region where water was, and is, in short supply.

In the 1950s, groundbreaking research by Fish and Game biologists identified the essential components of healthy streams: clean water, natural stream channels, and adequate in-stream flows. Using the existence of wild trout as their baseline for rating stream productivity, these biologists, in cooperation with the federal Bureau of Sport Fisheries and Wildlife, created a classification system to judge ecosystem health. Mapping their findings, the biologists colored the most productive, and thus pristine, waters blue. In

1958, the Yellowstone River became one of Montana's first "blue-ribbon trout streams," a designation that would help protect it and other "blue-ribbon" rivers long into the future.

Throughout the 1960s, rumblings grew concerning Montana's potential for energy development and the massive quantities of water that would be needed to support it. The Fish and Game Department would figure prominently in the subsequent battles over water allocations.

Historically, the consumptive use of water, especially for agricultural purposes, had ruled the day in Montana, but new national recreation studies revealed the growing popularity of and insistence upon the non-consumptive use of water for wildlife and human leisure activities. These studies also provided an opportunity for Fish and Game Director W.J. Everin to speak out. In his 1961-62 Biennial Report, Everin proclaimed:

"No other period of American history has witnessed as keen an interest in outdoor recreation as we are now experiencing. Outdoor activities are no longer considered as mere luxury; rather, they are gaining acceptance as an integral part of the nation's health and well-being." Then, in the same report, the Fish and Game Commission connected the dots for the legislature and for the public: "Fishing is an important part of tourism, which is of great economic importance to the state," and, therefore, "the Fish and Game Commission recommends the enactment of legislation designed to protect stream fishing habitat."

With the commission's blessing, the Montana Fish and Game Department launched a campaign to inform the public about how stream channel alteration, which would occur on a grand scale if water was diverted for energy development, would affect blue-ribbon trout fisheries. The Billings Jaycees heard Fish and Game's message loud and clear, and together they took their case to the state legislature, which in 1963 narrowly voted to adopt the nation's first Stream Conservation Act. Savvy proponents designed the act to expire after two years, temporarily assuaging concerns about government control and hoping the law's trial run would prove it less onerous than opponents believed it would be.

Between biennial legislative sessions, the Montana Fish and Game Department, the state Jaycee organization, and the Montana Wildlife Federation (MWF) redoubled their education efforts and, in 1965, secured adoption of a permanent law, renamed the Stream Preservation Act. This time, legislators overwhelmingly voted "yes," allowing Fish and Game and the citizen groups to tackle another issue: strengthening Montana's existing, but unenforceable, water quality law.

Energy issues continued to heat up and prompted the Fish and Game

Department in 1966 to create the Water Resources Development Section in its Fisheries Division, with Jim Posewitz at the helm. Three years later, the new water section morphed into the Environmental Resources Division, with Posewitz still in charge. The new division's broad task was to represent and defend the needs of fish and wildlife in the face of accelerating road construction, forest clear-cutting, pesticide use, water pollution, and strip-mining.

Don Aldrich, 1988.
Tawney Family Collection

By the time the 1969 legislative session convened, six months before the Sargents moved to Cinnabar Basin, Montana was under full siege by national and international energy speculators, including Western Energy, a subsidiary of the state's largest utility, the Montana Power Company. Corporate lobbyists prowled the capitol, eager to provide legislators with easy-to-digest facts skewed to promote all-out energy development. Some legislators agreed with these professional lobbyists and others fell hard for the corporate line, overwhelmed as they were by their responsibilities to complete the state's business—in every area—within a 90-day session. After hours, friendly and well-paid lobbyists welcomed these lawmakers to lavish hospitality rooms, replete with sumptuous buffets and bottomless beverages.

Into this atmosphere of corporate largesse, Montana's nascent environmental movement sent a single soldier, Don Aldrich, the executive secretary of the Montana Wildlife Federation.

Retired after 30 years as a lineman for the Montana Power Company, Aldrich lobbied in direct opposition to his old employer. His heroics cannot be overstated. All alone, with a no-frills expense account, Aldrich built a statewide telephone network, pumped out a weekly newsletter, and earned the respect of friend and foe alike for his honesty, earnestness, and ability to provide solid data and hordes of citizen lobbyists to counteract the well-funded corporate machines.

Aldrich's efforts brought results. In 1969, networking with local rod and gun clubs and the state Fish and Game Department, he helped win passage of critical amendments strengthening the Montana Water Quality Act. He continued to lobby for conservation during the 1971 and 1973 legislative sessions and during the 1972 state constitutional convention. With the unwavering leadership of Don Aldrich, everyday Montanans, for the first time, publicly questioned the wisdom of wholesale energy development and asked for mine reclamation, strict adherence to laws calling for clean water and clean air, and future financial support for boomtowns that inevitably would go bust. Tackling such complex natural resource issues was not for the fainthearted.

A couple of months after the landmark 1969 legislative session, with either impeccable or rotten timing, Leonard Sargent, who longed to retreat from the world's turmoil, brought his bride to Cinnabar Basin, not far from the epicenter of many fiercely brewing environmental battles.

Allenspur Dam was their first.

Political baptism

Busy settling into their new life together and soothing their blended family, the newlyweds sat out America's first Earth Day on April 22, 1970, an event that inspired a generation to speak out and take responsibility for Mother Earth.

Earth Day became Earth Year as the foreboding message of Rachel Carson's *Silent Spring* and other exposés of wanton pollution spurred passage of the National Environmental Policy Act (NEPA) and creation of the cabinet-level Environmental Protection Agency. NEPA quickly became Top Gun in the environmentalists' arsenal by requiring, for the first time, rigorous scrutiny of any activities that might affect air, water, and other natural resources. Environmental impact statements would provide thorough scientific and social research, as well as allow input from the public. Government decision makers would be required to use all these data to determine whether to authorize, deny, or demand modification of specific projects.

In 1971, Republican Senator George Darrow of Billings used the NEPA model to fashion the Montana Environmental Policy Act (MEPA), the state's cornerstone for sound decision making in a public setting. MEPA ultimately became law despite stiff opposition from Democratic Party leaders in Butte and Anaconda who claimed that too much protection of the environment would eliminate jobs. As former Democratic Congressman Pat Williams later explained, his hometown of Butte was suffering from a decline in the copper mining industry and "I'd have voted to build brick outhouses in the bottom of the Grand Canyon if I thought it would have provided good jobs."

Also in 1971, as Len and Sandy Sargent finished the extensive remodeling and enlargement of their rough-hewn cabin, a consortium that included the U.S. Bureau of Reclamation, 19 investor-owned utility companies, 6 rural electric cooperatives, 2 public power districts, and 8 municipal power suppliers, unveiled a bold plan to build 21 giant power-generating plants near coal mines in Montana and an equal number sprinkled across Wyoming, the Dakotas, and Colorado. According to the *North Central Power Study*, electricity generated by burning Montana coal in these power plants would travel west as far as Los Angeles via massive transmission lines. The coal itself would be shipped east by rail to Minnesota where it would be used to fuel midwestern power plants.

This quasi-governmental master plan had one big hitch: The 42 proposed mine-mouth power plants would require massive amounts of another resource—water—to produce the steam required for generating electricity or for converting coal to synthetic gas or liquid fuel. Where would developers find enough water in the semi-arid Northern Plains?

The answer came in the 1972 *Montana-Wyoming Aqueduct Study*. In this report, the Bureau of Reclamation identified sites for potential reservoirs, major and minor water conveyance conduits, as well as a host of specifics for delivering water to generate electricity or to produce fuel. In Montana, engineers resurrected 75-year-old plans to impound the Yellowstone River at a narrow mountain notch, naming their structure after a former Union Pacific whistle stop just south of Livingston, Montana. Designed initially to provide water for agriculture, Allenspur Dam would create a reservoir, 380 feet deep and 5 miles across at its widest, by flooding 31 miles and 32,000 acres of fertile Paradise Valley, the scenic and popular northern gateway to Yellowstone National Park. The impoundment would obliterate a 56-mile blue-ribbon stretch of the meandering Yellowstone, the longest free-flowing river in the Lower 48.

The Sargent Ranch nestled in Cinnabar Basin, not far from the southernmost end of the lake-to-be. For Len and Sandy, the honeymoon was over.

To Len, the scenario proposed by the *Montana-Wyoming Aqueduct Study* was all too familiar. Diverting one-third of the Yellowstone's average flow, as the study suggested, would render the river's lower reaches seasonally depleted and lifeless like the river that flowed near the orange groves of his grandmother and uncle in south-central Florida. Len had hunted and fished along the Kissimmee River since boyhood and mourned its loss when, in the 1960s, the winding river and its wetlands were harnessed for flood control by a deep-channel canal. With loss of the Kissimmee still fresh, Len reacted with passion to even a suggestion that Allenspur could solve the massive water needs of possible energy development: Damming another free-flowing river would be an "abominable crime," he asserted.

Joining with other concerned residents of Paradise Valley and its fringes, the Sargents formed the Stop Allenspur Dam Committee.

Hope and new mandates

Even in their outrage, the Sargents and others found hope in Montana's new constitution. Ratified in 1972, the constitution included very specific and heartfelt language proclaiming, "The state and each person shall maintain and improve a clean and healthful environment in Montana for present and future generations."

The carefully chosen words of Article IX and those of the document's value-laden preamble reflected the ability of a diverse group of delegates to put politics aside, a first for the deliberations of any governmental body in Montana. The 100 delegates came to their task free from the tangles of seniority fights and partisan bickering since, by law, none of them could be current legislators. Collegiality was further enhanced when the delegates chose to take their seats in alphabetical order, rather than aligning themselves by their respective political parties.

After the constitutional convention, many former delegates became legislators and brought their thoughtful and collaborative traits to the floors of the Montana House and Senate. Often these delegates-turned-legislators shared the concerns of the Stop Allenspur Dam Committee and of the statewide citizen groups springing up to meet the challenges of natural resource development. Among the new organizations were the Northern Plains Resource Council (1972), a coalition of ranchers and other citizens concerned about coal issues, and The Environmental Lobby (1973), a one-session, loose-knit advocacy group that broadened the work of Don Aldrich and the Montana Wildlife Federation. Supporting the majority of issues tackled by these upstarts was a coalition that included the MWF, state AFL-CIO, Montana League of Women Voters, Montana Farmers Union, low income and women's groups, and, of course, the Montana Department of Fish and Game (the agency's name in the early 1970s).

This broad and progressive coalition successfully lobbied the 1973 state legislature to enact landmark bipartisan legislation that directly and indirectly affected development of the state's energy resources. These important new laws included the Montana Strip Mining and Reclamation Act, the Major Facility Siting Act, the Resource Indemnity Tax Trust Act, and the Montana Water Use Act.

The Water Use Act quickly became a powerful tool for resource advocates. Historically, water law in this arid state held that to establish a valid right to water, water had to be put to a "beneficial use," which inevitably meant taking water out of a stream, whether for irrigating, providing drinking water, or filling a swimming pool. The Water Use Act authorized government to reserve in-stream water for new "beneficial uses," such as allowing adequate flows to meet the needs of fish and wildlife and to protect water quality. The law also established a system of adjudication, whereby claimants could seek to reserve water, but a judge ultimately would decide how best to allocate available water. Reservations would be made drainage by drainage, beginning with the Yellowstone River and its tributaries, where energy companies had been gathering water rights.

When totted up, the amounts required by the new beneficial uses of in-stream flow precluded the depletions proposed by the *Montana-Wyoming Aqueduct Study* and, ultimately, Allenspur Dam, which was the elephant in the room as the inevitable solution for massive water storage. The Water Use Act touched off what would become a 7-year battle over in-stream reservations of Yellowstone River water.

During one of the interminable government hearings over in-stream allocations, Leonard Sargent, with a face weathered by a lifetime of wind and sunshine, took the microphone: "I'm a rancher and an irrigator and I think we need to leave some water in these streams for the fish and the wildlife."

That was a statement that got some attention, especially in Montana. Before passage of the Montana Water Use Act, state doctrine allowed Montanans to take every last drop of water from a stream, even in a dry year. Now habitat preservation was a new "beneficial use" and when a rancher said, "Let's let the water run downstream with nobody using it," people listened carefully.

"It sort of brings you out of your stupor," recalled Jim Posewitz, who, as environment and information chief for the Department of Fish and Game, already had spent several years documenting the needs of fish and wildlife and, in the process, passionately working to keep the Yellowstone River flowing. Len's singular statement precipitated a long friendship between "Poz" and the Sargents.

R.I.P. Allenspur Dam (for now)

As the hearings continued, the volley of arguments exposed a fatal flaw at the Allenspur site. As luck would have it, the proposed dam lay directly over an active earthquake zone, not many miles from where, in 1959, a deadly tremor had collapsed a mountain, which buried 19 campers and dammed the Madison River, creating Quake Lake.

Nevertheless, energy developers continued to flood Montana's Department of Natural Resources with applications for water use permits. In response to this pressure, Governor Thomas L. Judge asked the 1974 legislature (meeting in the state's only annual session) to impose a three-year moratorium on major withdrawals from the Yellowstone River. The legislature granted the moratorium and effectively delayed action on industrial-sized diversions and impoundments, buying time for municipalities and state agencies, like Fish and Game and the Department of Health and Environmental Sciences, to comprehensively assess their own needs.

In July 1974, the Bureau of Reclamation issued a follow-up report on its earlier bombshells. The federal agency's conclusion, wrote K. Ross Toole in *Rape of the Great Plains*, was nothing short of astounding:

> ...It had been widely assumed that the study would simply affirm the bureau's a priori stance that the national energy crisis necessitated the stripping of western coal on a crash basis. That was, in effect, the stated policy of the White House in "Project Independence." It had clearly been the bureau's view as set forth in many documents, most notably, the *Montana-Wyoming Aqueduct Study*.
>
> But now the bureau had *some* of its data and its report reflected very serious doubts about the whole project. The reason? Water. Even with interbasin and interstate transfer, said the report, there was not enough water.

A few of the plants proposed by the *North Central Power Study* eventually were built and they found plenty of water for their needs thanks to the moratorium on major water diversions imposed by the Montana legislature. In the meantime, the United States multiplied its economy several-fold, and OPEC dropped its embargo.

By 1975, private energy corporations no longer quoted from the *North Central Power Study* or the *Montana-Wyoming Aqueduct Study*, and the government quietly let the studies gather dust. Yet, as environmentalists pointed out, the plans were never entirely abandoned, since Montana's natural resource agencies stayed busy processing a growing number of substantial mineral leases and water permit applications. Many of these resulted in public announcements and actual construction starts.

For the rest of their lives, the Sargents remained ever vigilant: "One of the problems," Len said, "is that 'wolf' has been called so many times, [the need for Allenspur Dam] has got to be well-documented. We're not playing dog-in-the-manger, everybody should recognize that, but how our resources are used will depend on what the state maintains" through strong legislation.

As the decade of the 1970s came to an end, the good guys had beaten back Allenspur Dam and the state had allocated 5.5 million acre-feet of water to protect in-stream values in the Yellowstone River and over 60 of its tributaries, but many more battles loomed ahead for Len and Sandy Sargent.

Hugging trees

Amid "many agonies redoing the kitchen (which is glorious, but log cabins aren't 'plumb'!)" and "an almost continuous stream of ever-so welcome guests from mid-May to mid-November (so-o many sheets, but we truly loved having every one!)," the Sargents, as their 1976 holiday letter suggested, were living at full throttle. A snippet read: "Our citizen activities/ concerns: Teton Dam disaster we fear only temporarily 'cooled' those bent on building Allenspur Dam in our valley—snowmobilers, etc., threaten our Beartooth/Absaroka Wilderness designation."

With Allenspur Dam reduced to background noise, the Sargents had discovered that another piece of their precious geographic neighborhood was under assault. This time, it was nearly 1 million acres of the Absaroka and Beartooth mountain ranges, southeast across the Yellowstone River from the Sargent Ranch and straddling the Montana-Wyoming border on the northern boundary of Yellowstone Park.

The two mountain ranges were a study in contrasts: The Absaroka featured high plateaus and deep canyons, dense forests and mountain meadows; the Beartooth rose in a panorama of rock and ice, sheltering fragile glaciers, spongy tundra, and icy lakes among its craggy peaks. In 1932, both landscapes received temporary protection by a progressive Congress as designated primitive areas, temporarily keeping at bay those who sought to mine, log, and build roads in their remote reaches. Official "Big W" (Wilderness) designation by Congress would permanently forbid such exploitation.

Thus, more than 40 years later, Montana Senator Lee Metcalf and others introduced a bill to establish the Absaroka-Beartooth Wilderness.

Congress scheduled a series of hearings in the affected region to gather facts and public opinion that would help lawmakers decide whether the primitive areas warranted permanent protection. In this new era, vociferous opposition spewed from the ranks of snowmobilers and people who liked to drive all-terrain vehicles in the backcountry.

Enter the Sargents.

Gordon Brittan, a philosophy professor at Montana State University in Bozeman, well remembers the time he, Len, and others carpooled to Big Timber, Montana, for one of the seemingly endless series of hearings. The small group of wilderness advocates wedged themselves into Big Timber's

high school gymnasium, already crammed to the rafters with dozens of
wilderness opponents. Many of the naysayers had come to support
construction of a road over some 60 backcountry miles, right through the
proposed wilderness and the northeast portion of Yellowstone Park.

From his official post at the front of the gym, Montana Congressman
Ron Marlenee railed against "tree huggers" and "prairie fairies," a
performance he often repeated on the floor of Congress where he also
lamented that poor old "Joe Montana, his fat wife, and his ice-cream-
smeared kids" would be shut out of wild places if they could not drive
through them. Speaker after speaker built on Marlenee's wild diatribe, their
attacks reaching a furious crescendo.

Finally, it was Len's turn at the microphone.

He began by disarming the crowd with his polite, signature
introduction: "My name is Leonard Sargent. I'm a rancher from Corwin
Springs." After momentarily milking a pseudo-bashful hick image, he
zapped his hostile audience in carefully measured words.

"He looked everybody in the eye and he just took off" explaining, in no
uncertain terms, exactly why the Absaroka-Beartooth needed and deserved
official "Big W" classification, marveled Brittan. Furthermore, Brittan said,
Len pointed out that Congressman Marlenee had "a lot of votes in this
room, but you're swamped in other parts of Montana and in the rest of the
country."

The boldness of Len's move is hard to overstate. Although night had
fallen, it was high noon in Big Timber as Len and the carload of wilderness
advocates took on a Congressman and a gym full of unruly wilderness
opponents.

After seven years as a Montana resident, Len knew full well that volatile
land use issues could trigger insane rage and some people might see gunplay
or lynching as a logical outcome. In a best-case scenario, he also knew that
the possibility of changing minds on the spot was nil. Yet, as a teacher, Len
believed that all people—even rabid anti-wilderness folks—were teachable.
And so Len did not mince words when he addressed Marlenee at that
hearing or later when he lobbied other Congressman one-on-one in the
nation's capitol.

Len and Sandy joined ranks with other members of the Montana
Wilderness Association and continued their crusade to protect the
Absaroka-Beartooth. Many more hearings in places like Big Timber and
lobbying trips to Washington, D.C, followed, culminating on March 27,
1978, with the official designation of the Absaroka-Beartooth Wilderness.

By then, Len and Sandy were seasoned conservation activists.

Access

The Sargents hardly had time to catch their collective breath when the Forest Service, from its headquarters in Bozeman, geared up a plan to punch an access trail through the Sargent Ranch to the swath of Gallatin National Forest that lay between the ranch and Yellowstone Park. Cheering on the government were public lands access groups, as well as hunters eager for a quick route to the abundant game animals that ranged on the national forest between the park and the Sargent Ranch.

The Sargents were outraged by the proposal, as Sandy made clear in their 1984 holiday letter to family and friends: "Our 'countretemps' [*sic*] with the Forest Service over their preposterous proposal to put access thru this 'de facto' wilderness buffer zone to Yellowstone National Park has permeated our lives this year incredibly and will again prevent any special trip this winter while we await their revised proposal and draft Forest Plan."

The annual letter went on to thank friends and family who responded to their pleas and wrote the Forest Service to support their position. Sandy warned that more letters might be needed: "This is a critical part of the Greater Yellowstone Ecosystem (which is being battered from all sides), and it behooves us all to 'Overcome'!"

The Sargents had learned to solicit help from the heavies, noting, "numerous organizations, people and Congressmen seem to be working hard for our 'cause' in the Washington arena." To provide ammunition for these friendly decision makers, Len and Sandy had hired wildlife biologists to collect solid data about the animals that roamed the Sargent Ranch.

For his part, Len threw the public access argument right back in the face of the public agency, arguing that its proposal would give scofflaws a direct route to trespass and poach grizzly bears on the Sargent Ranch. Further, Len told the Forest Service, the country adjacent to the ranch was a whole lot of straight up and down, so the agency could expect falls, accidents, and, likely, some deaths. Saving people involved in mishaps inevitably would require search and rescue operations, endangering other lives. What would the government want next? A road for all-terrain vehicles and logging trucks?

By the end of the decade, distracted by bigger resource issues, the Forest Service essentially abandoned its effort to provide public access through the Sargent Ranch, giving Len and Sandy a de facto "win."

Had this been a real conservation battle? Even their closest friends could see that the Sargents' argument against public access stemmed more from human nature than from a desire to protect grizzly bears and alpine country. Friends privately recognized that Len and Sandy had fallen victim to the

NIMBY (Not In My Back Yard) syndrome and wanted to protect their personal sanctuary.

New Age, new neighbors

In 1981, a new and unexpected adversary came on the scene. The Church Universal and Triumphant (CUT) purchased the 12,000-acre Royal Teton Ranch right next door to Len and Sandy. As true believers in a blend of eastern religion with the apocalyptic aspects of Christianity, the well-heeled sect immediately announced plans to make Malcolm Forbes's former haven its world headquarters, where thousands of CUT followers could await the rapture of the Golden Age prophesied by their leader, Elizabeth Clare Prophet.

Heeding Prophet's vision, CUT also bought property in tiny Corwin Springs so that its holdings lay on both sides of the Yellowstone River and included the bridge and the only road leading to Cinnabar Basin. A group of fresh-faced, hardworking CUT followers soon moved to Corwin, where they refurbished the Spanish-style buildings of a long-ago dude ranch and opened a café, serving organic vegetables raised in CUT's massive, state-of-the-art greenhouse. They assembled a large and impressive array of road-building and farm machinery, which they cared for in outsized storage sheds and barns. And they filled expansive pastures with cattle and sheep, fencing out the bison, elk, and other animals that migrated annually from Yellowstone Park.

Friendly to each other and to sanctioned guests, CUT members closely guarded every corner of their self-sustaining compound and extensive property. Aquarian-Age sentinels kept particular tabs on everyone who traveled to Cinnabar Basin and made certain that none turned up a side road along Mol Herron Creek, a Yellowstone River tributary leading to the mysterious sacred site where thousands of CUT followers gathered annually.

The omniscient presence of the passive-aggressive sect clearly rattled the Sargents and their Cinnabar Basin neighbors, as well as other folks who owned properties interspersed with CUT's string of holdings along the Yellowstone River. Since Cinnabar Basin Road was their only ranch access, Len and Sandy were careful not to offend Elizabeth Clare Prophet or CUT, and they never made public statements about their discomfort or mentioned it in holiday letters. However, less vulnerable neighbors were vocal and adamant opponents of the wealthy and litigious sect. These folks documented any false move by CUT and appealed, in vain, for government help.

But at last, some of CUT's activities were too flagrant for the authorities to ignore. The state health department discovered petroleum from a leaky storage tank had contaminated an area adjacent to Mol Herron Creek, where massive underground bomb shelters were being built in anticipation of a millennial apocalypse that would usher in the prophesied Golden Age. The National Park Service was up in arms when CUT drilled a well to access Yellowstone's geothermal plumbing for energy and hot water. Then, in 1989, the sect ran into real trouble when the federal government convicted and imprisoned Elizabeth Clare Prophet's husband, Ed Francis, and another CUT member for conspiring to buy hundreds of automatic weapons and ammunition.

As the millennium neared, CUT's legal troubles and its leader's early diagnosis with Alzheimer's disease took a toll on the number of sect recruits. Fewer prospects were willing to turn over all they owned to a shaky organization whose "Messenger of the Ascended Masters" was clearly losing her mental faculties. Upon his release from prison, Ed Francis and others filled the leadership vacuum and began looking for a way to resolve CUT's financial dilemma. Short on cash, the group turned to its investment in land.

At the southernmost end of the ranch, just below a geologic landmark known as the Devil's Slide, stretched a grass and sagebrush flat where CUT had planned to build an Aquarian-Age town. The proposed site also happened to be historic winter range for bison, elk, antelope, and mule deer. Other parts of the ranch provided crucial winter range and migration corridors for grizzly bears and Rocky Mountain bighorn sheep.

Monitoring CUT's flagging finances, the Rocky Mountain Elk Foundation (RMEF) stepped in to help broker a deal between CUT, RMEF, the Forest Service, and the U.S. Department of the Interior. Multiple transactions ultimately preserved 7,850 acres of habitat through a complicated package involving land exchange, outright acquisition, and conservation easements.

Len and Sandy liked RMEF, a national organization established in 1984 to preserve wildlife habitat, not only because of its mission, but because their dear friend, Phil Tawney, had helped RMEF get started and grow into a well-funded and sophisticated outfit. As the organization's private counsel, Tawney had initiated negotiations on the CUT property and, when he died prematurely in January 1995, Len and Sandy gave RMEF $100,000 to establish the Phil Tawney Fund, as part of the nonprofit's Northern Rockies Habitat Fund.

The Sargents knew RMEF had the expertise and the moxie to pull together a complicated deal like the one Tawney had begun on the Royal Teton Ranch, so they earmarked a portion of their generous gift to help RMEF bring all the players to the table. The results were typical of how the

Sargents operated: Find good people, give them what they need, then stand back, and let them run.

Len, Sandy, and Phil Tawney all had passed on by 1998 when the deal was finalized, but a sign near Corwin Springs commemorates their generous commitment and dedication to habitat preservation. In 2000, the Cinnabar Foundation honored the RMEF executives who completed the complex negotiations with the Royal Teton Ranch—Ron Marcoux and Gary Wolfe—with the second Len and Sandy Sargent Stewardship Award. The award had been established a year earlier at the recommendation of Sandy's son Rick Hubbard Sargent to honor the memory of his parents and to recognize deserving individuals for outstanding conservation achievement in Montana and the Greater Yellowstone Ecosystem.

As the new millennium arrived without the apocalypse predicted by Elizabeth Clare Prophet, large ungulates made their hard-wired journey southward from Yellowstone Park to winter on protected ground. By then, the Church Universal and Triumphant had unraveled and most of its resident members had drifted away. And peace once again returned to the neighborhood encompassing Cinnabar Basin and the narrow Yellowstone River Valley.

Jim Posewitz, center, presents the Len and Sandy Stewardship Award to Gary Wolfe and Ron Marcoux of the Rocky Mountain Elk Foundation, 2000. *Gayle Joslin.*

Timing is Everything

Pat Williams

Good manners and good instincts gave Len and Sandy Sargent a leg-up as they became advocates for the natural resources of their adopted home. Maturity also played an important role as they interacted with savvy politicians. Experience had taught Len and Sandy that to make a political—or any—point, they had to show up at the right time, and they had to know what they were talking about. With a potent combination of manners, maturity, and experience, backed by a fat pocketbook, the Sargents earned the attention and respect of the powerful in Helena and in Washington, D.C.

Former Congressman Pat Williams was particularly impressed with their exquisite timing. Etched in Williams's memory is an instance that occurred in the late 1980s while Congress considered the Montana Wilderness Bill, which would bestow official wilderness status on federal roadless areas already identified as worthy of permanent protection by the 1977 Montana Wilderness Study Act, sponsored by Montana Senator Lee Metcalf. Williams's omnibus bill, long sought by the Montana conservation community, would have forever banned logging, mining, and motorized vehicles from 1.4 million acres of the state's wildest public lands.

Writing a complex wilderness bill required a philosophy of pragmatic benevolence, a strong sense of economics, and the ability to keep a moist finger constantly aloft in the political winds. Shepherding such a bill through Congress required nerves of steel.

Timber and mining interests accused bill sponsors of picking industry pockets, and skeptical conservationists asserted that the sponsors already had climbed into those same pockets. Meanwhile, members of the disparate groups fired off scalding letters to other Congressmen, who helped or hindered the bill's progress, according to input from their own constituencies and campaign donors.

Presenting his omnibus wilderness bill to a packed committee room, Congressman Williams was taking shots from all sides when he spotted Len and Sandy, standing along the back wall. Their unexpected presence lifted his spirits.

"I gave them a little wave...so they knew I'd seen them," he remembered. "They hadn't called for an appointment, which they usually did when they came out (to the nation's capitol). They simply wanted to be at the hearing and talk to me afterwards."

When the hearing was over, the Sargents were waiting to speak to their Congressman.

"Walking (back to my office), they shared with me in very specific terms, without notes, the changes they thought the bill needed," the former lawmaker marveled. "Neither one of them dominated the conversation. They both knew their stuff."

Lobbyists and constituents constantly buttonhole Congressmen, but this encounter with the Sargents stuck in Pat Williams's mind.

"It had to do with timing," he explained, "influencing something at precisely the moment it is to be influenced." Lobbyists, whether corporate or nonprofit, earn their bread and butter by mastering such timing, "but with the Sargents," Williams continued, "they were individuals, just common citizens who learned to leverage their influence with fairly exquisite timing, and they also knew what they were talking about. Nothing influences politicians more than good, accurate information. Facts. And the Sargents always knew their stuff."

Len and Sandy employed that strategy throughout their busy lives: Show up at the right time and know what you're talking about.

The Yellowstone River
Cinnabar Foundation Collection

CHAPTER 3
The Perfect Conjunction

We the people of Montana grateful to God for the quiet beauty of our state,
the grandeur of our mountains, the vastness of our rolling plains,
and desiring to improve the quality of life, equality of opportunity
and to secure the blessings of liberty for this and future generations
do ordain and establish this constitution.
– Preamble to the Constitution of the State of Montana, 1972

Len's first brush with the tangled politics of Allenspur Dam taught the prep school teacher a tough lesson: Government, which he once had pledged to defend under any circumstance, was not infallible. The admiral's son and former Navy officer realized he could no longer be a blind loyalist. To his chagrin, Len began to share the fervor of youths who continued to protest long and loud about government policies gone haywire.

Len's feisty wife already understood more about government and policy-making from her perspective as single, working mother: "I say that politics enters your life with the garbage truck." Fascinated by government and politics since her Westover days, Sandy was more than ready to dive in.

As the Sargents waded into the morass of natural resource issues facing Montana and the greater Yellowstone area, they found themselves surrounded by idealistic young upstarts, and they were not a bit uncomfortable. After all, the Sargents had dedicated their lives to young people—Sandy, to her own kids and those she encountered over the dozen years she worked in church and school settings; Len, of course, to his students at Taft, where for 30 years he had lived among them, taught them, coached them, and spent summers with them.

As a friend observed, young people may have disappointed both Sargents for a while, but neither Sandy nor Len could walk away from them.

Joining the fray

Clutching a brand-new Ph.D. from the University of Michigan, Bill Bryan arrived in Montana in 1972 to begin life as an environmental advocate in the Northern Rockies. With few contacts here or in Idaho and Wyoming where he also planned to work, Bryan looked up his old hockey nemesis, Len Sargent. It wasn't an easy call for Bryan to make, since he remembered Taft's Winter God as "the picture of arrogance" during the early 1960s when he played hockey for rival Hotchkiss School.

The Hotchkiss alum never guessed he'd be received so graciously by the former Taft School coach. No longer facing off across the ice, the two became fast friends, although whenever Bryan visited the ranch, Len always made sure they dined on fine china embellished with scenes from The Taft School.

Len and Sandy provided a sounding board for Bill Bryan in his new work. As Bryan made his way through the tangled web of issues facing the region, he met other young environmental activists and introduced them, in turn, to the Sargents. And that is how my husband Phil Tawney and I became lifelong friends of both Bryan and the Sargents.

At age 24, my husband and I already were caught up in the politics of Montana conservation, having been recruited by Don Aldrich, the state's only conservation lobbyist, to join him during the 1973 Montana legislative session. Broadening our constituency base beyond the Montana Wildlife Federation, the group Aldrich served as executive secretary, we called ourselves The Environmental Lobby. We raised funds to cover our expenses and spent long hours lobbying and keeping conservationists throughout the state informed about and involved in the legislative process.

As the session wound down, we knew that increasingly complex demands would threaten Montana's natural resources during the next legislative session, which would come around in just nine months (the 1974 session was Montana's only experiment with annual sessions). Brainstorming in the basement of the little house we rented as The Environmental Lobby, Aldrich, my husband, and I, along with Bill Bryan and several MWF and Environmental Lobby supporters, concluded that environmentalists needed a year-round organization to properly monitor and lobby for natural resource issues at the state level. We took our idea to a larger ad hoc group and, in December 1973, founded the Montana Environmental Information Center (MEIC). MEIC's first board of directors included Len Sargent, and later he became MEIC president.

MEIC hit the ground running, with Phil Tawney and me as its first staff members and a host of support from volunteers. The 1974 legislature passed its three-year moratorium on major diversions or impoundments in the Yellowstone River, denied coal companies the right of eminent domain, and considered land use legislation to further control rampant subdivision in pristine places. The latter was of keen interest to Len as he began a three-year term on the Park County Planning Board.

With Len, you also got Sandy, and when the legislature met again in 1975 and 1977, they loaded their bulky station wagon with casseroles and retrievers and moved to Helena for the state's biennial tug of war. During both legislative sessions, they rented a comfortable furnished home suitable for entertaining legislators as an alternative to the hotel suite hospitality offered by high-salaried corporate lobbyists.

In the 1970s, mature and committed volunteers like the Sargents were absolutely critical. It was a time when many Montana environmental advocacy groups were just organizing and the average age of their collective staffs was 24. With nary a thought about age, Len and Sandy worked side by side with staff leaders young enough to be their children. As consummate MEIC volunteers, they personified good manners that compelled like behavior. They generously offered much-needed financial support to help build a solid foundation under what rapidly became one of the state's most effective and committed conservation groups.

Every week during the 1975 and 1977 legislative sessions, Sandy stayed up past midnight typing labels and stuffing envelopes for MEIC's *Capitol Monitor*. Much of that newsletter included information garnered from Sandy's meticulous notes, written in her efficient shorthand during countless legislative debates and committee hearings. In addition, she kept MEIC's growing files in order, posted agendas, tracked bills, and reminded harried young activists to balance their typewriter carriages properly, à la the Katharine Gibbs School. As staff godmother, Sandy also sewed on buttons, wiped chins, and gently offered her less-than-subtle observations about wardrobes and haircuts.

As for Len, he put young and old at ease with his genuine interest in their lives and viewpoints. He offered sage advice to young lobbyists and affably swapped stories with rancher-legislators of all stripes. Len testified repeatedly on a variety of issues, always introducing himself in that familiar way: "My name is Leonard Sargent and I'm a rancher from Corwin Springs."

Len's effectiveness as a lobbyist is hard to judge. His participation probably helped—often he was a rancher talking to other ranchers—but neither his testimony nor his buttonholing clearly affected the outcome of any particular bill. In a state where citizens could walk right into the governor's office and call him by his first name, Len stood out as a "gentleman" rancher who fancied his herd of exotic Limousin cattle. He was not a "real" rancher whose livelihood depended on how well he grew grass and black Angus calves, but he was a card-carrying member of the Montana Stockgrowers Association, American Cattle Association, Montana Farmers Union, National Farm Organization, and Montana Limousin Association. Len raised cattle, but falling beef prices never gave him night sweats.

Conservative lawmakers rightly pegged Len as wealthy, well educated, and from "back East." Because of his pedigree, some of them—maybe a lot—dismissed his liberal and frequent testimony as the ramblings of an out-of-state drugstore cowboy. Ironically, those same legislators listened carefully to the well-paid three-piece suits representing Plum Creek Timber of Seattle, Burlington Northern Railroad of Minneapolis, the Anaconda Company of New York City, and other out-of-state corporations. These cagey national and international corporations hired native sons as their frontline lobbyists—men who enjoyed long-standing relationships with legislators and other community leaders.

The Sargents understood the nativistic streak of Montanans and they understood the value of perspective, of knowing that bad things can happen to beautiful places.

As Len reflected: "I've always felt that one reason I'm so concerned about what's happening in Montana and this area is because I've seen what's happened in La Jolla [California], where it used to be nothing but a little, tiny restaurant with the sawdust on the floor and people saying, 'Oh, wouldn't it be wonderful for two or three people to build here.' Ha! It's solid buildings. I think that people who have always lived in Montana have a very important perspective, but they are missing not knowing about what could happen here and what may be happening here. It makes you more sensitive to conservation issues."

The Sargents also understood the importance of personal relationships. During their two winters in Helena, Sandy spent Sundays in her rented kitchen, whipping up and freezing lasagnas and tasty desserts that could be defrosted later in the week to woo or comfort weary legislators and the inevitable clutch of young lobbyists. Many lawmakers found the Sargents' home cooking and conversation welcome substitutes for the restaurant steaks and free-flowing cocktails offered by the hired guns of corporate America.

White hats and hostess skirts

While intimate dinners helped solidify legislative support and foster a feeling of community, once each session, Len and Sandy took their notion of entertaining many notches above the ordinary. From 1977 to 1997, the

Sargents hosted biennial White Hat parties for a veritable who's who of good guys—progressive-minded legislators, other elected officials, and sympathetic lobbyists—at the Montana Club, the inner sanctum of those who wore black hats. Sandy came up with the name, and she chose the setting.

Designed by Cass Gilbert, architect of the Woolworth Building in New York City, the Italianate limestone monolith rose six stories just a block off Last Chance Gulch, Helena's main street and the site of a major gold discovery in 1864. Since the early 1900s, the Montana Club, like any other metropolitan gentlemen's club, had been an elegant watering hole (and residence in its early years) where power-mongers lingered to plot and scheme about controlling Montana's electoral process and to divvy up the profits they reaped from plundering the state's natural resources. Through the polished hardwood doors was a world inhabited by the descendants of nineteenth-century cattle barons and railroad kings, mine speculators and whiskey traders, utility company executives and politicians. A perfect venue for the Sargents' White Hat Party.

Unlike lavish corporate soirees, where vulnerable legislators became easy prey for conniving lobbyists, the White Hat Party provided a chance for like-minded people to mingle while savoring fine wine and an exquisite buffet, surrounded by people who appreciated what they did and told them so. Sandy planned everything with the detail of a debutante's coming-out party or southern cotillion, right down to the full-length skirts she wore and insisted that I and a few other women also wear "so the guests know who the hostesses are." It was a rare night indeed for young environmentalists working the trenches at starvation wages.

The White Hat Party was equally out of the ordinary for state lawmakers, people who could be wined and dined almost every night of the legislative session. The hosts of this party were not asking for personal favors or preference or pork. Instead, the White Hat Party was a great big "atta-boy" to the environmental movement and to the legislators who supported the green cause.

The Sargents' gracious and simple strategy worked. Their dressy party became a not-to-be-missed biennial pep rally for conservationists and let the White Hat legislators know they had lots of friends.

Role models

Len and Sandy Sargent, educated, articulate, and generous with both time and money, had found a new calling in Montana as godparents to the state's nascent environmental movement. They provided year-round leadership through example, moral support, and, with their boundless tenacity, they shamed people decades younger into enduring long and tedious meetings.

The Sargents exhibited remarkable grace in 1979 when, after years of service, Len was denied another term on MEIC's board of directors. He essentially was slapped in the face by the organization that he and Sandy had nurtured from its beginnings as benefactors and volunteers.

The insult to their largesse came about during a brief period when, as the Sargents' friend Bill Bryan remembered, the MEIC board was dominated by people "who didn't want anything to do with people with money." According to Bryan, "Len was not, from their point of view, politically correct enough. He was kicked off the board because of who he was. And there was a board in the first place only because of who he was." Those board members eventually moved on.

Despite the harsh treatment, the Sargents remained loyal to MEIC and its many causes, and like the gentleman he was, Len kept his hurt feelings to himself. Eventually honored with MEIC's 1990 Conservationist of the Year Award, the Sargents never retaliated, never spoke a bad word about the organization, or tolerated badmouthing by others. And they continued to support MEIC generously.

The snow could be hip-deep in Cinnabar Basin and the thermometer might climb as high as zero that day, yet, right after breakfast, Len would grab a shovel and start digging out the driveway. Then he would chain up the station wagon and climb the steep pitch to the ranch road and there Len would stop, load the retrievers, and Sandy would hop in. Together they would plow through ice-crusted drifts and slide through canyon bottoms never kissed by winter sun. When they finally reached the paved and snow-packed highway, Sandy would take over and drive the remaining 60 or 200 or 300 miles to their destination.

Such was a routine day for Len and Sandy, retired folks who were plenty old enough to say, "No thanks, maybe next time." Their long and harrowing drives to virtually any meeting or government hearing eliminated any excuses that other people might have had for not showing up.

"In your worst moment, it was sort of an embarrassment," remembered Tom Roy, another former MEIC board president who also mentored young people as a volunteer activist and director of the Environmental Studies Program at The University of Montana. "Leonard and Sandy are going to be there, so I'd better be there. In its more positive aspects, it showed people that, by God, this is what it's really about. Commitment."

No matter how far they had to drive, the Sargents arrived smiling at each event and they stayed until the bitter end, knowing full well the kind of roads that lay ahead of them. By their example, Len and Sandy raised the bar for activists of all ages, gladly doing whatever was needed with open hearts and open wallets, and left an undeniable imprint on the environmental movement in Montana.

"They had an ability to inspire young people to become leaders in the environmental movement," said Jim Jensen, MEIC's longtime executive director, "and they did that by the example they set in how they led their lives, and their participation in our civic life, with their wonderful sense of humor and just tremendous optimism and upbeat outlook on life and on Montana. They had an abiding love for this place. It was infectious."

Building organizations to last

In the mid-1970s, Montana environmentalists were creating organizations for the long haul and, by default, inventing careers in activism that provided full-time work, a plethora of experiences and skills, and, hopefully, enough money to pay the bills. Many of what would become Montana's bedrock environmental groups faced constant financial crises in those early years, times when a few hundred dollars meant the difference between closing doors or being around to fight another day, another season, another year. Len and Sandy were unfailingly generous.

"Their financial contributions made it possible for these organizations, certainly MEIC, to become credible," Jensen asserted. "We wouldn't be here but for Len and Sandy Sargent early on, helping to nurture the ideas and the people that made these organizations work."

The Sargents truly cared about each and every activist who gave body and soul to the environmental movement, and they were not afraid to show it.

As Tom Roy said, "If you or I were across the room and she [Sandy] spotted us, she'd come running over and give us a hug. And then we'd be off to the races together."

And you'd both know the course. The Sargents helped make sure of that.

"They took their lives seriously and they didn't waste their time," Jensen said. "They also, I think unconsciously, imposed a high standard on all of us: to be well informed, to participate in a thoughtful and constructive way."

Environmentalism was "their life, their passion, their muse," explained their son, Rick Hubbard Sargent.

Len and Sandy invigorated MEIC, they helped create the Greater Yellowstone Coalition, and they were key supporters of the Northern Plains

Resource Council and the Montana Wilderness Association, all critical watchdogs and participants in the ongoing environmental battles of the state and region. The Sargents carried many individuals over stumbling blocks that might have ended or radically shifted promising careers in the green movement. They bought meals, and they covered bad checks. They ushered their young friends through marriages and births, breakups and divorces, and deaths. They took activists into their home for weeks at a time, letting them sleep late when they were exhausted, and rousing them early when deadlines loomed. They became surrogate parents to many in the environmental movement and surrogate grandparents to their offspring.

Recalled Roy, "Here these young folks were, young and inexperienced, without any real legitimacy except their enthusiasm and commitment, at a time in Montana's environmental history when the soil was most fertile for things to take hold. And you've got Leonard and Sandy moving to town. It's just kind of the perfect conjunction. There was really a sense of adoption that took place."

Over time, protecting Montana's wildlife and wild places became an important part of the state's economic fabric, making it possible to build a career in the environmental movement by continuously garnering experience and honing skills. Today, many organizations pay decent wages that cover mortgage payments and college tuition for the next generation, thanks in no small part to the early, generous contributions of the Sargents—funds that helped those same groups keep the lights on and the staffs paid.

Len, speaking to the Montana Wilderness Association.

Jumpstarting with greenbacks

For Placer Dome, it was business as usual. Despite opposition, the Canadian mining giant proceeded with plans to expand its Montana gold mine, perched high above the Jefferson River and Interstate 90 between Butte and Bozeman.

The company's Golden Sunlight Mine already ranked among the world's largest cyanide-leach, open-pit gold mines when, in 1988, it received the go-ahead from the U.S. Department of the Interior to expand operations on the property it leased from the Bureau of Land Management (BLM). The federal permit flagrantly ignored Article IX, Section 2, of the Montana constitution: "All lands disturbed by the taking of natural resources shall be reclaimed."

What's not to understand in that carefully crafted sentence? Without proper reclamation, a constitutional requisite in Montana, toxic compounds from the Golden Sunlight expansion could eventually seep downhill and into the aquifer that fed the Jefferson River and the potable wells of nearby Whitehall.

To avoid disaster, in 1990 the Montana Environmental Information Center and four other conservation groups registered a formal complaint with the U.S. Interior Board of Land Appeals. In its decision, rendered more than two years later, the federal board agreed that the mine's meager plan was deeply flawed and increased Golden Sunlight's reclamation bond. The board failed, however, to require adequate reclamation.

Matters became stickier in 1992, when Placer Dome assumed ownership of the property supporting its Golden Sunlight operation through a land trade with the BLM. That trade put the Montana Department of State Lands in the driver's seat since reclaiming private holdings was a state requirement.

Jim Jensen knew that the only way to avoid catastrophe was to get to court fast. From his hot seat as MEIC's executive director, Jensen knew that only a lawsuit would force the Department of State Lands to comply with Montana's constitution and reclamation laws. With Placer Dome now poised to begin its expansion, speed was of the essence, but none of the five plaintiffs—MEIC, National Wildlife Federation, Mineral Policy Center, Gallatin Wildlife Association, and Sierra Club—had the wherewithal to launch what would surely become a complicated and lengthy lawsuit.

Catching wind of MEIC's need, Len Sargent quickly jump-started the legal fund with a $5,000 gift, and the lawsuit was filed. Once again, Len's timing was impeccable. Moreover, his donation opened many other wallets.

A gnarly fight ensued, resulting in several decisions by state District Court Judge Thomas Honzel, including a landmark 1994 ruling that ordered the Department of State Lands to prepare an environmental impact statement and declared unconstitutional a section of Montana's hard rock mining reclamation law that exempted open pit mines from reclamation. The protracted legal battle spanned more than 15 years, eventually reaching the docket of the Montana Supreme Court where State Lands and the company appealed a 2002 ruling by Judge Honzel that required the mine's open pit to be at least partially backfilled. Then, in a bizarre twist, they asked to withdraw their appeal. The Supreme Court denied their move for dismissal. A decision on the appeal has yet to be released.

Clearly, the 1992 lawsuit and Judge Honzel's subsequent decisions avoided a nightmare of environmental consequences to the Jefferson River and the sleepy town of Whitehall. That critical lawsuit, Jensen asserted, "only happened because Len Sargent understood the importance of the case and was willing to invest some degree of faith in MEIC."

In 1999, Jim Jensen received the first Len and Sandy Sargent Stewardship Award for his leadership on mining issues in Montana. His letter of recognition cited his efforts to influence the regulatory process, assure compliance with constitutional guarantees, require adequate reclamation, and prohibit failed technologies.

In accepting the award, Jensen acknowledged that his success was, in large part, due to the Sargents.

CHAPTER 4
The Ranch

There is a balm in Cinnabar Basin that makes the wounded whole.
– Sanna Porte, inscription in the Sargent Ranch guest book, undated

Almost from the beginning of their married life, Len and Sandy were caught up in the conservation and politics of their adopted state and region. Naturally inquisitive and gregarious, they opened their home and their hearts year-round to Montana's environmental activists. Unless the Sargents' visitors lived in Gardiner, nearly 20 miles away, stopping by or answering a formal invitation to dinner usually meant spending the night at the ranch. In 1976 alone, nearly 70 people signed the guest book.

Continuing the habit he had begun with his Taft crew, Len tried to convince his new friends that they were helping him run the place. By the back door of the ranch house stood a row of tall rubber "guest boots" in a variety of sizes so visitors could keep their feet dry while accompanying Len and Chevy, Poupee, Tubby, or Cinnabar on their rounds, feeding Zeke and the rest of the horses, nominally checking the irrigation system, but mostly showing off the ranch.

All comers were welcome, despite the endless rounds of cooking, laundry, and cleaning that fell mostly on Sandy's strong shoulders. In the evenings, the Sargents and their guests would shower and change into dinner clothes: sportscoats (Len wore a Harris tweed and a silver bolo) or clean shirts for men, and skirts, or at least dress pants, for women.

The Sargents' very civilized cocktail hour was carefully scripted to appear nonchalant, giving Sandy the time she needed to finish dinner preparations. An hour before dinner, Len poured the drinks—for many of us, Len and Sandy's personal favorite, gin and Schweppes' Bitter Lemon—and started the cheese tray on its path around the living room. Meanwhile, the aproned hostess remained sequestered in her kitchen, putting together the meal between sips of her own highball and, until she quit smoking, puffs of a cigarette. (In the early 1990s, Sandy finally gave in to pressure from Len and Rick to live a longer, healthier life for her grandchildren; by then, Len had been smoke-free for 20 years.) When guests offered Sandy assistance, she chased them out with a wave of her hand and a cheery "go on!" Too many helpers, especially unfamiliar ones, spoiled her routine. Besides, happy hour at the Sargents demanded their guests' full attention; many an issue was thoroughly dissected and strategy created before the hearth at the Sargent Ranch.

Blessed with exceptional hearing, Sandy put everyone to shame with her supreme ability to multitask. Two rooms away from the living room, above the clatter of pots and pans, the beep of timers, and the drone of the ever-present kitchen TV, she could hear every word of conversation and made sure she was heard, as well. While dinner simmered gently on the stove, smoke and fire spewed from the kitchen as Sandy served up biting comments about spineless politicians, greedy corporations, and shirking bureaucrats. Some guests, mellowed by Len's potent drinks and soft couches after a day afield, had trouble matching Sandy's venomous diatribes, let alone the verbal gymnastics of a multilayered discussion.

With the most current environmental problems solved or at least examined, it was time to eat. While Len poured the wine, Sandy enlisted help to fill the dining room sideboard with her casseroles or roasted meats, vegetables du jour, and scrumptious salads. Then, on cue, guests would load up the fine china, take their assigned seats, and wait. Only the untutored or someone with a significant lapse in judgment had the nerve to dig in before their hostess came to the table, responded to the inevitable toast, and lifted her fork.

Throughout the dinner hour, the Sargents' black Labrador and golden retrievers and any guest dogs lay immobilized on the Oriental rug gracing the living room hardwood. Having supped even before cocktails, they were the height of doggy decorum with their blissfully full stomachs and never begged or even raised their heads.

Cocktail ruminations that had spilled over to the dinner hour slowed as the humans, too, felt the effects of a good and hearty meal. When all the human guests were sated, Sandy and a trusted family member or friend would clear away the dishes and do the kitchen chores. No cleanup was complete until all the food-smeared plastic storage bags had been washed and draped inside out on the drain board by the sink.

With everything tidy once again, Sandy and her helper would rejoin the party in the dining room for coffee and a delectable dessert. Then, it was back to the living room for a nightcap and more conversation. At last, Sandy would relax, curling up on her favorite worn floral couch with her latest needlepoint project, and elicit talk of matters more personal and

The Sargent Ranch

Sandy and Len

Cinnabar Mountain

comforting, readying herself and everyone else for a good night's sleep.

At bedtime, Len accompanied the dogs on their final evening outing. He supported all of Montana's natural predators, but he did not want the ranch pets to be somebody's midnight snack.

The Sargent Ranch became a Mecca for conservation activists—a luxury retreat with a five-star restaurant, capably managed by Sandy with only occasional help. The Sargents provided a safe, out-of-the-way haven where the heady mix of dead-serious discussions with calming food and soft beds rejuvenated the most battle weary. But more importantly, earnest young activists felt unconditionally appreciated and accepted by people of their parents' generation because of a shared passion for and commitment to the natural world.

"When you went to the Sargents," recalled longtime friend Bill Bryan, "you got your tank refilled. You did it in little vignettes, here or there with Len, or with Sandy out in the kitchen. And you came away feeling, this is okay, this thing I'm doing."

Over 20 years, besides providing R&R for individuals, the Sargents welcomed state and national conservation groups for board meetings and retreats in their spectacular, off-the-beaten-path setting. While Sandy saw her role as chief cook, hostess, and pit bull, Len saw his as host and facilitator, often introducing like-minded people and giving them the opportunity to explore their commonalties and work together. Len particularly relished mixing green youths from Montana with seasoned veterans from San Francisco or Washington, D.C., tossing in an idea or two, and then letting things cook.

Len and Sandy became the hub of a vast network of conservationists and like-minded public officials, and they usually had the latest news about any breaking issue. During their first 10 years on the ranch, the Sargents maintained their far-flung connections to family and friends via a party line they shared with seven other ranch families. A common inconvenience of life in a remote area, the eight-party line meant: 1) neighbors had to wait for a clear line to dial, and 2) anybody could pick up the phone and listen to someone else's conversation.

"That was a trip for my mother, who loved to talk," Rick chuckled. And, I would add, liked to have the inside scoop on everything.

In the late 1970s, to the relief of all, the Sargents and their neighbors celebrated the advent of single-party phone lines.

Retired, but not retiring

Between guests and long-distance calls, Len and Sandy became familiar and expected faces at local, state, and national hearings on natural resource issues, and at an endless string of events sponsored by politicians and conservation groups. They jumped into life in conservative Park County, renowned for its opposition to land use planning and anything that smacked vaguely of control. In 1974, with the fervor of an environmental evangelist, Sandy paraded her beliefs in a race for county commissioner and received a thorough trouncing on Election Day.

"She wasn't real tactful," recalled her son, "and politicians need to kiss people on both cheeks."

Two years later and undaunted, Sandy won a seat on the constitutionally mandated Local Government Study Commission. Commuting 60 miles one way from the ranch to Livingston, she worked fervently for a new county charter that emphasized public participation, open meetings, and shortening the terms of county commissioners. After a year of meetings, the local government group presented its charter, which Park County voters defeated. Interviewed a few years later, Sandy noted one of the ironies of the election's outcome: "After everyone screamed that [implementing] the charter would be too expensive, the commissioners got three pay raises."

From 1973 to 1977, Len had his own brush with local politics as one of 16 county residents appointed to the Park County Planning Board. As expected in a county of property rights advocates, Len usually found himself alone in his quest for a land use plan to control the sundry developments cropping up in the fertile Paradise Valley. Old-time ranchers, content with their isolation and the rugged individualism it spawned, fought any initiative that might infringe on their ability to subdivide or otherwise control activities on their land.

Lock step with the conservative attitudes of his constituents, Pete Story, a long-serving state senator, once told me: "We can't turn Montana off to save a few goose nests." As a respected descendant of pioneer stock, Senator Story led the charge to defeat land use planning at every level of government.

The lack of a land use plan in their home county and the defeat and manipulation of state legislation that could restrict subdivision development rankled the Sargents for more than 25 years.

"You can't stop people from moving in because [Paradise Valley] is such a wonderful area, but if some initial planning doesn't go on, they're going to end up sorry they moved here," Len reflected. "You can have people move in if you do it right. If you don't have any plans or any long-range thinking, then you are in trouble. The reason they can get thousands of dollars an acre instead of $30 or $40 an acre is partly because [the Yellowstone's] a beautiful river and it's beautiful land surrounding it. If they don't have some sort of sensible planning down the line, they are cutting their own throats financially. Their land will not be worth much. At the moment, the growth, the pioneer spirit of 'this is my land and I can do anything I damn well please' is not only wrong, it's shortsighted."

Sandy summed up their position: "I'm afraid there are too many people who are not thinking ahead and are not realizing what they're doing is destroying why they live here and why they've come here."

"They don't care," Len added. "They've already got the money and they can leave."

Paradise Valley and the rest of Park County continued to attract more and more developers and celebrities, déjà vu for Sandy because of her experience in Vail. As newcomers locked up large tracts of land for subdivisions, hodgepodge developments, and private sanctuaries, the locals finally and begrudgingly agreed that maybe a comprehensive land use plan was not such a bad idea. Still, old habits die hard, and it took decades before a countywide plan was formally adopted.

Preserving sanctuary

In the meantime, the Sargents had made sure that their earthly paradise would forever remain virtually unchanged.

Working with MEIC and other groups in 1975, they successfully lobbied for legislation enabling landowners to protect their property in perpetuity through voluntary conservation easements. Through these legal agreements between landowners and qualified organizations or government agencies, landowners may permanently limit property use to preserve the conservation values of open space and wildlife habitat. Voluntarily relinquishing certain rights is considered a charitable contribution and qualifies a landowner for significant tax relief in the form of reduced income, estate, and/or gift taxes. A conservation easement travels with the deed in perpetuity, whether the land is later sold or bequeathed to an heir.

In 1979, The Nature Conservancy (TNC) settled into its new Montana office. The first piece of business for Executive Director Bob Kiesling was accepting a donated conservation easement on the Sargent Ranch. In their easement, Len and Sandy covered all the bases they could, allowing historic agricultural use and forever prohibiting subdivision, most new buildings, the use of off-road vehicles for recreation, all commercial hunting and game farms, and the hunting of bears and bighorn sheep.

Len and Sandy relished the fact that environmentalists and
agriculturists could find common ground in voluntary conservation
easements that preserved ranchland, because, as Len liked to point out,
easements were "something you can talk about without inflaming tempers."

Audacious advocacy

The Sargents continued to ruffle feathers when they felt it could make a
difference. Appearing before Congress and on network TV, Len spoke up
for grizzlies and against bison hunting, and promoted the return of wolves
to Yellowstone National Park. In 1982, he joined the board of directors of
the Natural Resources Defense Council (NRDC). Highlights of these
activities, as well as the Sargents' work with MEIC, the Montana Wilderness
Association, and the League of Women Voters, received mention in Sandy's
holiday missives, which never failed to shamelessly promote issues and
admonish recalcitrant politicians. A cryptic and often caustic summation of
the Sargents' current conservation battle ate up one-third to one-half of the
one-page, single-spaced, typed letter. The 1982 Sargent letter took to task
those who were slow to evolve:

> ...Some friends chided us for including "politics" in our
> letter last year. Howsomever [sic], we find (perhaps because
> we live in a large and sparsely populated state where it's
> constantly visible) that such affects almost every aspect of
> one's way of living, habitat and world—economically,
> environmentally, socially, judicially, philosophically, etc.,
> etc.—all of which encompass the true meaning of
> "environment"—the totality of the world in which we live,
> move and have our being. Whatever one's persuasions, we
> cannot help but feel that spiritually we are charged to do
> our best as "good stewards" to leave this world a better
> place because of our privileged presence. Thru what
> avenues is up to each individual, but should not LOVE
> instead of GREED be the overiding [sic] guide and
> foundation? We rejoice at the increased "involvement" of
> churches thruout this crazy, often mixed-up world of ours
> and pray the spirit of brotherly love can ring out loud and
> clear and bring all nations and people to "cooperation"
> instead of "confrontation"! "We have not inherited the
> earth from our fathers—we are borrowing it from our
> children."

Occasionally, Sandy used the annual letter to teach a lesson in ecology.
For example, when the fires of 1988 annihilated wide swaths of Yellowstone

Park and threatened the Sargent Ranch, Sandy explained how fire played an important and natural role in the ecosystem and defended the National Park Service for its burn policy. Or when a grizzly bear tore a hunk of siding from a new outbuilding and cruised the lawn for sweet clover, she tied this exceptional and destructive behavior to the impact of the ongoing drought on the bear's natural foods.

And always, the Sargents found humor in their good or occasional misfortune. Their attendance at meetings and family gatherings sometimes produced striking contrasts and fodder for a good laugh: One June, while Len suffered through 90-degree heat at an NRDC board meeting in New York, Sandy tried to plant her ranch garden in the snow. In September that year, it was Sandy who melted while visiting relatives in New York's sweltering 90s and Len who frantically wrapped pipes in a 15-degree cold snap back at the ranch.

Every letter from the Sargents, whether personal or the mass-produced holiday annual, concluded with a hand-scrawled note and an invitation to visit the ranch.

Setting boundaries

With national and "local" meetings, and the flurry of guests coming and going, the Sargents had to leave their ranch to recharge. Trusting their affairs to a series of able winter caretakers, Len and Sandy visited relatives on both coasts, attended Elderhostels that featured diverse classes from Dancercise to constitutional fathers, and toured the world, often on special eco-education excursions, expanding their circle of friends—friends they never failed to invite to the ranch. So large was their circle, they seldom traveled without seeing someone they knew—former Taft students or other friends who provided red-carpet tours.

Whenever the Sargents returned from their travels, they barely had time to unpack before guests began to arrive once again.

By 1987, the constant company was taking its toll, especially on Sandy, so the Sargents built a three-bedroom, two-bath caretaker's cottage. A married couple, Lil Erickson and Phil Herne, became the Sargents' first and only year-round caretakers, helping Sandy with endless mounds of laundry, housecleaning, and meal preparation; and helping Len with maintenance of the main and guest houses. The Sargents regarded Erickson's commitment to conservation issues as a bonus and provided her with a computer and the time, space, and encouragement to pursue her own activism.

In 1992, leaving the ranch in their caretakers' able hands, the Sargents made a second trip to Africa, this time taking Rick and Judi to celebrate Rick's 40th birthday. There, Len and Sandy suffered a rare disappointment

Len reads *The Night Before Christmas* to Kerri and Calley, 1986.

The family's 1991 holiday photograph, taken at Rick and Judi's home in Santa Barbara. *Back row, left to right:* Rick Hubbard Sargent, Calley Hart, Len, Trip Hart. *Front row, left to right:* Judi Stauffer, Sandy holding Grace Hart, and Kerri Hart holding her youngest daughter, Taylor.

when some friends they had expected to see were absent, having already left the Continent to attend international conferences elsewhere. Even then, there was consolation, as Sandy gleefully wrote in a postcard from Tanzania: "Ran into John Craighead [the famed Yellowstone grizzly bear biologist] at river log jam and twice since—such a small world."

The next year, the Sargents stayed closer to home: "We didn't take a big trip," just "10 days on a superbly converted mine sweeper in the Inland Passage of Alaska with a very special group from the Sierra Legal Defense Fund;" home for 18 hours to repack for a week's tour of Montana Indian reservations; then, "left that group before dawn to fly to San Francisco for a family wedding (we'd mailed out clothes earlier!)." Of course, close friends and family always knew the latest Sargent itinerary, which Sandy unfailingly distributed, with its minutiae of personal contacts, phone and fax numbers, and addresses.

The Sargents' dance card continued to be filled almost year-round and whole weeks during the summer months. They were so welcoming, in fact, only especially close friends could be denied their hospitality. Susan Cottingham recalled a time when she phoned Sandy from Helena, contemplating a weekend of rest and relaxation at the ranch. Susan knew she had arrived in the inner circle when, after pressing the issue, Sandy leveled with her: The timing wasn't good.

Such an admission was not easy for Sandy, the penultimate hostess, yet she was comforted whenever good friends recognized that she and Len had had enough company and needed time for themselves. Even with Erickson's help, Sandy was clearly exhausted by the steady stream of guests. Listening by phone to her week-by-week recitations of summer plans, I could sense tiredness and a feeling of entrapment in a place meant for getting away.

Moving on

Beginning in 1985, the Sargents spent much of each winter near their son Rick and daughter-in-law Judi's home in Santa Barbara, California. When the opportunity arose "suddenly" in 1988, the Sargents bought a second home there as a "good insurance policy." Sandy gushed about their new "cottage at Valle Verde, a delightful retirement complex in Santa Barbara, which we'll use off and on for at least several years to come."

As bona fide senior citizens, the Sargents had become increasingly concerned about living so many miles from emergency medical care in their isolated Montana basin. Also, the long drive from the ranch to the nearest towns and airports had become a bit daunting as they maintained their busy schedules around the state and around the world. Something had to give. With their conservation easement in place, Len and Sandy reluctantly decided to sell their beloved ranch. "We know the ranch, number one, won't be purchased by someone who doesn't want to maintain it," Len said at the time. "We know whoever owns it from now on will keep it the way we've always had it."

Not quite ready to give up country life, the Sargents purchased bare land on Jackson Creek, midway between Livingston and Bozeman, where they planned to eventually build a passive solar home. In 1993, for a "temporary pied-à-terre," they bought a two-story condominium in Bozeman, their selection sealed by a family of ducks that frequented the stream meandering near the unit's tiny deck.

Daughter-in-law Judi Stauffer cherished her time with Len on what would be a last trek to High Lake, "finding joy in the smallest aspects of nature" as they looked over the ranch. A conservation buyer had been found and, by the following year, the ranch sale would be final.

While Len and Sandy recognized the inevitability of the move from their hallowed basin, the move itself was gut-wrenching. The 1993 holiday season was bittersweet as the entire family of children and grandchildren gathered to celebrate their last Christmas and Len's last December birthday on the ranch. On Christmas Eve, one of their last remaining horses, Perky, died of old age. After the holiday break, Kerri and Trip took their daughters home to Issaquah, Washington, and Rick and Judi left for Santa Barbara. Rick returned to the ranch shortly after the New Year to help pack up and move more than a quarter-century of accumulated possessions—a labor of love that took more than three months. Judi rejoined the family for the move to Bozeman.

As Len and Sandy drove out of Cinnabar Basin for the last time, they left behind the graves of Zeke, Perky, and the other ranch horses, as well as the graves of their Labrador and golden retrievers, including their last dogs Cinnabar and Bib (Black Is Beautiful). Driving down the dirt canyon road in a final, solemn caravan with his parents and his wife, Rick said, "I had a lump in my throat trying to hold back the emotions of leaving 'the last best place' I'd known."

The Sargents crammed their favorite artwork and prized possessions into the three-bedroom Bozeman condo, a space too small to entertain as they normally would. Acknowledging how different their lives would be without the ranch and their spacious home, Sandy focused on the positive: "There are times for everything in your life. With the Paradise Valley changing so much, I'm glad I don't have to drive it anymore."

In fact, both Sandy and Len reveled in attending "many events we used to have to skip" and going to movies on the spur of the moment. They were swept up by the bustle of political and cultural activity in the New West college town of 40,000, becoming patrons of the Bozeman Symphony Orchestra and the Museum of the Rockies. What had been a two-hour drive to downtown Bozeman became a 20-minute walk. In a true mulligan, Len took up golf again after a 50-year hiatus.

The Sargents looked forward to designing their eco-friendly home on the town's outskirts, but when Sandy was diagnosed with leukemia in 1995, it became clear that Bozeman and Valle Verde would be their only homes. As Sandy confided to me in a letter, "I think Len has finally realized (tho' not adjusted to) that R&J [Rick and Judi] will eventually be the ones to build at Jackson Creek—whew!"

Still, Len remained a bit wistful: "Feeding ducks beats feeding cows, but I miss having the dogs around."

Their first Christmas in Bozeman also was very different. Instead of trekking up a snowy slope and sliding the annual Christmas tree home on a toboggan, the Sargents drove to a local nursery like other city dwellers and bought a tree. Sandy presented Len with a life-sized concrete sculpture of a golden retriever, sitting and staying, like all his goldens, beside his favorite chair. From then on, whenever Len sat in that chair, he automatically rested his hand on the "dog's" solid head, finding comfort in its familiar form.

While the Sargent Ranch provided fond memories for two generations of prep school students and for legions of family, friends, and organizations, it was critical in shaping the Sargents' views of Montana, politics, and conservation. The way Len and Sandy used their ranch, both as a working ranch and as a gathering place, epitomized their fundamental tenets: live well, but limit your impact; share what is dearest to you; and help your friends to do their best work.

The Sargents had preserved their land's natural amenities through a conservation easement and they had nurtured a growing environmental movement. When they sold their ranch, Len and Sandy ensured their philanthropic legacy by giving the proceeds to the Cinnabar Foundation.

Len and Sandy died within five months of each other in 1997, after a marriage of nearly 28 years, most of it spent on the ranch. Len always joked that he waited a long time to marry Sandy because he wanted to make sure she would turn out. She did.

And so did their ranch. They made sure of that.

Old Zeke

Commitment to place

During the bulk of the 1960s, the Sargent Ranch had been an oasis of a different sort throughout the unpredictable, high-altitude summers. The drafty homestead cabin provided shelter and little else to Len and his clutch of Taft School ranch hands. With no central heating and not much in the way of plumbing, the rustic accommodations matched the wild western landscape of Cinnabar Basin, making a stay at the ranch a coveted experience.

While nearly all of Len Sargent's prep school helpers discovered something about themselves and left the basin tanned and fit, some young men found even more. Barnaby Conrad III, a Yale University student and Taft alum like his father, was older than the rest of the crew when he arrived at the Sargent Ranch in 1972. He came to the ranch after a chance encounter with Len in San Francisco. Nearly paralyzed by grief over the recent loss of his mother, Conrad told his former teacher and mentor that he needed something, though he was not quite sure what that "something" was. Len listened, with understanding. Then they talked about their common heritage as descendents of Montana pioneers, and Len invited the bereaved young man to come "home."

At the Sargent Ranch, Len put Conrad and the Taft teens to work for four days each week, building a Quonset hut, digging postholes, and fixing fences. During their days off, Conrad and the boys sometimes rode horseback to a tiny, crystalline lake in nearby Yellowstone Park, where they would creep to the water's edge and catch native cutthroat trout with their bare hands. After they had had their fill of grabbing fish, the crew would jump into the lake, splash around a bit, and then hightail it back to the ranch, drenched and happy.

Eight weeks of hard work and untethered play amidst wildlife and wild landscape soothed the sad and searching soul of Barnaby Conrad. More than 30 years later, the respected author and editor still cherished the memories of his healing summer in Yellowstone country—its dense forests full of elk and bears, its ragged mountain peaks dusted with fresh snow and dotted with bighorn sheep.

Whether Len knew it at the time, with every carload of Taft students he hauled west and every work crew he invited to the ranch, he was creating a unique constituency for Yellowstone Park and the area surrounding it. Like Barnaby Conrad, many of the impressionable young men, and later women, remembered their summers in Cinnabar Basin, and they remembered them fondly. They might forget about the sting and itch of horseflies and mosquitoes and the discomfort of dust and prickly hay clinging to sweat-drenched skin. But who could forget how a live trout felt as it wriggled free through your fingers; or how, early one morning, you scared up a majestic bull elk that snorted its irritation in frosty plumes; or how the sight of fresh grizzly bear tracks in the mud sent shivers up your spine?

These experiences cement a person to place. And, from their gentle teacher, Conrad and the other ranch hands learned that such places are rare indeed in a modern world.

When the Sargent Ranch alumni finished their formal education and built successful careers, Len tapped their summer memories and introduced those with financial resources to environmental groups that needed their help to protect the very amenities they remembered.

The Cinnabar Foundation founders:
Len and Sandy Sargent,
Phil Tawney, and
Jim Posewitz.

CHAPTER 5
Two Kinds of Green

*To every man there comes that special moment when
he is tapped on the shoulder and offered the chance to
do a very special thing.— Winston Churchill*

Both Len and Sandy were reared in the upper middle class with modest family inheritances, but they continued to live comfortably as adults because of their own hard work and careful savings. As a divorced mother of two, Sandy spent many years working full time and wisely managed her earnings, which enabled her to build her little chalet in Vail before that Colorado mountain town became outlandishly chic and expensive. For most of his life, Len received a small stipend from a media company founded after World War II by his father and a maternal aunt's husband, Payton May. Living a Spartan life in a Taft School dorm, Len carefully set aside his inheritance and much of his schoolteacher's salary to build the nest egg he used to purchase his ranch.

Not rich by today's dot-com standards, but financially secure, the Sargents were generous in donating their money and their time. When they moved to Cinnabar Basin and learned about the complex issues facing their adopted state and the Greater Yellowstone Ecosystem, Len and Sandy dug deep and offered their support. Word of their generosity and commitment quickly spread among regional environmentalists, and many beat a hasty path to the Sargents' door. Few walked away empty-handed.

Longtime activist Bob Kiesling recalled, "He [Len] had this notion that he could do best by spreading dollars around here and there in the organizations whose missions he admired, but more particularly among people he had relationships with. He was a strong believer in the power of vigorous and well-meaning people to get out there and make a difference."

The Sargents' first personal gifts ranged between $1,000 and $5,000, but sometimes they gave as much as $10,000 to earnest young activists and upstart advocacy groups. Accumulating wealth was never a goal for Len and Sandy. They lived well, but not extravagantly, and they had a lot of fun giving away money.

"The thing we've been particularly pleased about is how tremendously helpful $1,000 or $2,000 can be to a grassroots organization in this area," Len once said.

Added Sandy, "We like to spread it around."

Only their accountant, Ernest Turner, knew that the Sargents gave away far more than 10 percent of what they earned through their investments. "A lot of people will tithe [donate 10 percent of their earnings] to their church, and they do it because it's a requirement of their religion," Turner said. "These people gave because they believed in the causes. And they gave to an extent far beyond what people would consider to be a normal charitable or donative amount of money."

Sometimes, a hard-luck individual or shaky organization would pick the Sargents' open pocket. Len was an especially soft touch, easy prey for a passionate activist who might claim his or her organization would be doomed without an immediate infusion of cash. Jim Posewitz remembered how Len willingly wrote a personal check for $2,000 to save a "flat-ass guilty check-kiter from jail because the guy had tried hard to save some grizzly bears, but lacked the skill to manage both his money and his organization." And then, Posewitz said, still with a bit of wonder, "When the check-kiter had the gall to come back around, Len gave him another handout."

An uncommon case, but not unique.

"Most of it [requests for personal assistance] was not evil intent," Posewitz said. "Some of those people had the passion, but they didn't have the technical competence, maybe."

With an accountant's sharp eye for numbers and a businessman's natural wariness, Turner was less generous: "Some of them were not reputable people. [They were] con artists who were using environmental activities as a way to support themselves."

Len rarely acknowledged his gullibility, but occasionally, after a particularly bad judgment call, he would tell Turner, "I didn't do so good on that one, did I?" Then Len would add sheepishly, "But he's a good guy."

Almost without fail, if someone like the check-kiter abused Len's trust and had the nerve to hit him up again, and Len believed that person was at least trying hard, the rascal would walk away with another check.

"Leonard Sargent was one of the best people I've ever met," Turner said. "He was unassuming, and he cared about people and he cared about the environment. He believed you. Even if you took him, he still believed that you probably meant well, and he might even help you again."

Building a foundation

Len and Sandy also believed that people with means who lived outside the greater Yellowstone area would share their love for the region and would want to help fund a charitable organization that directed donations to grassroots environmental groups. So in 1975, the Sargents brought together like-minded souls from Montana, Wyoming, and Idaho with professional fundraisers from both coasts. Meeting at the Sargent Ranch, those assembled laid the groundwork for the Northern Rockies Foundation, reflecting the Sargents' vision of a regional foundation that could get the most bang for its bucks because it "knew which groups were doing what in the ecosystem," as Sandy explained.

The Northern Rockies Foundation made only a few grants and disbanded within two years.

"Unfortunately, we got the wrong executive director who used up all the money without raising any himself," Sandy explained. "[By then] we had done a lot of fundraising on both coasts and in between. We had a feeling for what was out there."

In 1983, still certain that grassroots environmental groups could benefit from a regional foundation, the Sargents decided to start their own and named it after the "best spot" Len had discovered so many years before. They gave the Cinnabar Foundation $10,000 in seed money and a promise to ultimately endow it with proceeds from the sale of the Sargent Ranch. Len asked his close friends, Jim Posewitz and Phil Tawney, to serve with him as members of Cinnabar's board of directors. They agreed to fund deserving nonprofit environmental advocacy and education groups, and conservation research in Montana and the Greater Yellowstone Ecosystem. Grants would be made from one-half of the interest earned on foundation investments and would be awarded in two categories, special projects and operating funds. The latter category would allow grant recipients to determine how best to spend the funds they received.

Funding operational grants reflected an important facet of Len and Sandy's philanthropy: Keep the rent paid and the lights on, and the troops fit and fed to do good work. As full-time MEIC volunteers in the mid-1970s, the Sargents learned firsthand that most funders shied away from making grants with no strings attached and preferred to support special projects with measurable results. Yet Len and Sandy knew that a nonprofit organization needs stable funding for overhead and administrative costs to carry out its projects and its mission.

Early Cinnabar Foundation board meetings convened at the Sargent Ranch toward the end of Montana's big game hunting season, and they did not last long. "We'd turn that 20 minutes worth of board work into three days of elk hunting," laughed Posewitz.

In 1985, the Cinnabar Foundation made its first grants—a whopping total of $1,123—to two lucky organizations, MEIC and the Great Bear Foundation.

The next year, Posewitz reported, "Len told us that he had put a substantial amount of money into the foundation since he saw no reason for us to have all the fun after he was gone." The "substantial amount" turned out to be $1 million, enabling Cinnabar to give away a total of $70,000 to 11 organizations. Bigger numbers meant it was time to get serious and add a fourth member—a treasurer—to the Cinnabar board of directors. Financial whiz Ernest Turner was the obvious choice.

As Cinnabar's coffers grew, Posewitz, Tawney, and Turner spread the word among environmental groups that they were to direct their funding requests to the Cinnabar Foundation, not to Len and Sandy. As Posewitz pointed out, "Any time you're giving away money, you have way more people looking for it than you've got money to give away." And Len hated to see people walk away with nothing.

"Leonard served as the [board] chair, but he also served as the guy who picked up the shattered pieces of good ideas that we just couldn't fund," Posewitz said. "He would always pick up the remains and say, 'I'll see if I can't do something about this.'"

That "something" invariably meant writing a check from his personal account, which he continued to do for the rest of his life. Sometimes he would write a personal check when, in his capacity as a board member, he had voted against funding a project.

Later, Len would go to his accountant with a joking request. "He'd say, 'Can I have an allowance?' I've been in this business for 40 years, and I've never seen another person like Len Sargent," said Turner.

Making more, giving more

By the late 1980s, Len's family firm in Virginia Beach owned small newspapers, radio stations, and television stations across the South. The company's equity had been divided into shares among family members, and those shares had been divided again among successive generations. The company was worth a ton of money, but paying a pittance of dividends per year. As Turner explained: "When you have a small position in a privately held company, you have basically nothing. It's not saleable."

However, just owning shares of stock provided an opportunity. Since its shares had been divided so many times, the company was almost "public," which would allow shares to be traded on the open market. To retain family control, the firm's managers decided to do the reverse of a public offering and keep the company private. Good news for the Sargents, their accountant said, because the family-owned media conglomerate offered to buy Len's shares for millions of dollars. Len happily accepted this new infusion of cash as a way to help more people do good work.

So it happened, in 1988 at the ages of 75 and 64, Len and Sandy Sargent went from very comfortable to rich. Despite the windfall, the Sargents did not ratchet up their lifestyle. "They might have gotten a new car," Turner recalled, "but it was a Subaru. They were Subaru people."

What the Sargents did do was get serious about giving away more money.

"This area is so incredibly beautiful and fabulous," Len once reflected. "There [are] an awful lot of things that need to be done so that our grandchildren can still appreciate [it]. Unfortunately, people don't think about their grandchildren as often as they think about their immediate pocketbook.... I'm sure this doesn't apply to [everybody] but money and wealth are so important now that people feel that they have to be able to prove how rich they are by putting the biggest house on top of the tallest hill, which is pathetic."

Sandy echoed their common passion: "Use that money to do some good."

The Sargents' savvy accountant and financial adviser explained further: "Money was just something that was there to pay bills or to help fund all the charities he was involved in, causes that he cared for. Money itself was no big thing. It didn't matter. It didn't make the slightest bit of difference to him that he had more money now than he did earlier, except that he could give more."

When the Sargent Ranch sold in 1994, Len and Sandy made good on their promise and donated the proceeds to the Cinnabar Foundation. By 2007, the foundation had $10.4 million in assets, due both to the Sargents' generosity and Turner's careful management. Cinnabar shuns investments in major polluters—"It doesn't make sense to invest in somebody who is doing the things that you don't want to do," explained Turner—and aims at earning 10 percent a year, reinvesting half of all earnings and distributing the rest to nonprofit environmental organizations.

With this investment strategy, Cinnabar's assets should double every 12 to 14 years, according to Turner. While Cinnabar will never be on a par with giants like the Gates Foundation, it always will play a significant role in the environmental movement of Montana and the Greater Yellowstone Ecosystem, giving away more money all the time, allowing groups to do their work.

And that is precisely what Len wanted it to do.

"He knew what he was building," said the Sargents' accountant. "He got Cinnabar built. It's there and it's solid, and it doesn't rely on anybody. Look at the end result. He got it."

Montana and the area around Yellowstone Park were not the only recipients of the Sargents' generosity. For the last decade of their lives, Len and Sandy spent several happy months each year at their California retirement home. They embraced life in Santa Barbara, quickly becoming a part of the Valle Verde community and socializing with people their own age who shared similar backgrounds and travel experiences. With the same zest for activism and philanthropy they displayed in Montana, the Sargents supported local environmental projects, including the Douglas Family Preserve, and delighted in attending and providing financial assistance to art exhibitions, concerts, theater productions, and lecture series.

Sandy and Len, 1990.

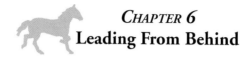

CHAPTER 6

Leading From Behind

When you can lead from the rear you've got it made.
— Len Sargent, from an interview by Scott McMillion, 1994

Leonard and Sandy Sargent embraced all of life's experiences—good and bad. They squeezed something positive from every corner of their lives and wisely turned even the toughest lessons into opportunities for growth and learning.

As Len reflected in 1995, "I'm awful [*sic*] lucky. I liked my prep school; I enjoyed Princeton thoroughly; I enjoyed the ranching. I particularly feel lucky to have been in World War II, because I don't think there was ever a period before or after where the country was more absolutely unified in what we were doing."

By way of illustration, Len told a story about a logger who went to Seattle and volunteered to help repair some of the ships damaged at Pearl Harbor. After the fellow failed to pick up three or four paychecks, the paymaster tracked him down. "[The logger] made, I think, an incredibly important statement," Len said admiringly. "He said, 'I won't take money to do the right thing for my country.'"

Sandy shared this expression of patriotism and an unwavering commitment to do right by her country. Like Len, she celebrated their generation's unified spirit during the Second World War when, despite the horror of the battlefield, Americans began to have a "sense of the world as one unit when they had to go to England and France, some in Italy and Africa, all those places," she said. Traveling, meeting people, and becoming acquainted with the cultures and the geography of foreign lands helped make the world a smaller place for those soldiers and for the Sargents.

Len and Sandy never stopped expanding their own worldview, even as they found new careers as environmental advocates. They took a hands-on approach to wildlife and wild land issues in Montana and the greater Yellowstone area, across the nation, and around the globe. The Sargents treasured the friends they made even more than the victories won.

They understood that some bad ideas just would not go away. "One of the scary things from the point of view of protecting the environment is that when we win a battle, it's wonderful, but the same threat could come up again 1 year, 10 years, 50 years down the line," Len said. For example, the Sargents related how they had tracked down an old friend from 25 years earlier. In the mid-1970s, when Montana was threatened with no-holds-barred energy development, the three fought alongside with the Northern Plains Resource Council, the Montana Environmental Information Center, and other groups. When Len, Sandy, and Carolyn Alderson met for the last time in the mid-1990s, their conversation went instantly to the Tongue River Railroad, a bad idea in any year. But the old friends had thought this idea was dead long ago. Not so. Energy scions still plotted to build the railroad right through prime agricultural land along the scenic Tongue River, shortening the distance from coal mine to coal-fired power plant, but not by much.

"We thought we'd buried [the issue] forever," Sandy lamented to Alderson who, as a rancher in the 1970s, had been in the thick of the battle. "So here we go again," Sandy reflected. "It's just amazing how these bad pennies keep popping up."

Then Len weighed in: "I don't think the issues have changed. There's just been an awful lot more of them. The issues go way back before most of us were in a position to help."

Even though the Sargents often found themselves confronted by a new barrage of old issues, they were not without hope. After all, Len pointed out, sometimes people say "Enough!" as they did over the channelization of his beloved Kissimmee River in south Florida. Len commended Congress for finally pressuring the Army Corps of Engineers to "put it back the way they found it." Restoration of the winding river and its wetlands finally began in the late 1990s, more than 30 years after the Corps had built its deep-channel canal.

"Hopefully, Congress will undo some of the [other] bad mistakes, some of which were done with good intentions," Sandy said graciously. "It's just that the science of the moment was wrong."

The Sargents' perspective and willingness to forgive environmental transgressions hearkened from experience. They loved being in the middle of things as leaders and advocates in Montana's emerging environmental movement. They cherished memories of the hubbub and flurry of those early days. "When we started in the 1970s," Sandy remembered, "there were probably 100 of us statewide. Here's the fourth largest state in the union, and we'd all race to everybody's problem—Northern Plains [Resource Council], taking care of the eastern part—and on and on, and we all would go barreling back and forth."

Barreling back and forth across the nation's fourth largest state with other activists who could've been their kids.

To the end of their lives, the Sargents continued to enjoy getting together with friends to reminisce and plan new strategies at the annual meetings of organizations like the Montana Wilderness Association (MWA). "The nice thing about it was that it gave us a chance to see a lot of our friends from all over," Len explained. "It's kind of like a college reunion, except we have even more in common." Sandy recalled that probably close to 30 couples "carried on every year" at MWA conventions.

The Sargents celebrated the boon in collaboration among different interest groups, especially conservationists and agriculturalists. "It's foolish they have been at odds because they really want the same thing—preservation of green space," Sandy said. The Sargents placed the blame for antagonism among the disparate groups squarely on the shoulders of many of their executive directors. "I think it's the executive directors wanting to keep their jobs," Sandy said. Added Len, "The best way to increase your membership is to have something that scares the heck out of them, so [people] join even if the scaring isn't legitimate."

The Sargents were heartened by the exchange of ideas and perspectives that took place when environmental groups sat down with local officials. For example, in pursuing its mission to advocate for sound resource policy in the Yellowstone ecosystem, the Greater Yellowstone Coalition (GYC) brought together representatives from each of the region's governmental entities: two national parks, two national wildlife refuges, six national forests in three regions, two Indian reservations, and 13 counties within portions of three states. A GYC board member at the time, Sandy recalled that one of the official representatives in attendance remarked, "Well, it's the first time we've been asked to meet." All of the meeting's attendees thanked GYC for bringing them together to discuss common problems and to brainstorm solutions in a collaborative and nonpartisan setting, Sandy remembered, emphasizing the importance of listening, learning, and keeping an open mind.

For 30 years, the Sargents shared their old-fashioned values with a host of nonprofit groups and individuals. Many of the organizations they supported are now mainstream, respected forces and the young people who originally staffed them are in midlife. Some, like Jim Jensen, MEIC's long-serving executive director, still lead the charge. Others, because of family obligations and fiscal necessity found more lucrative careers, but stayed involved in other ways as board members or elected officials, or both.

Facing new challenges

Len and Sandy kept on the move in 1994. In July, they once again joined a World Wildlife Fund expedition to Africa, this time visiting Botswana and Namibia with Kerri and Trip Hart to celebrate their daughter's 40th birthday; in October, they viewed polar bears in Churchill, Manitoba, with the Great Bear Foundation. In between the Sargents' far-flung adventures, they worked on various Montana political campaigns and pressing issues. After the November elections, they celebrated the Oregon wedding of Sandy's sister Sabra to Jack Cleveland, and dashed home to Bozeman to spend the holidays with family before heading to Santa Barbara for the winter.

The Sargents had barely arrived at Valle Verde when they were off again: to Helena where they hosted their biennial White Hat Party and then to New York City for a sneak preview of Dinosaur Hall renovations at the American Museum of Natural History, a GYC-sponsored event. In February, Len and Sandy joined my children and me in Albuquerque at the annual convention of the Rocky Mountain Elk Foundation (RMEF), where they were recognized publicly for their generous gift to RMEF in honor of my husband, Phil Tawney, who had succumbed to acute myelogenous leukemia six weeks earlier.

After Albuquerque, the Sargents dashed off to Bozeman, cruised through the Panama Canal, and landed back in Santa Barbara and Valle Verde, where Sandy's annual physical exam put a hitch in their plans for the second half of 1995. A routine blood test alerted Sandy to myleodysplasia, a pre-leukemia condition that caught the Sargents completely by surprise. When a California oncologist balked at trying to cure a 74-year-old woman and told Sandy to get her affairs in order, the Sargents made a beeline back to Montana, as Sandy later wrote, "for treatment by a superb doctor," the oncologist who had treated my late husband. Following a textbook progression, Sandy's pre-leukemia soon morphed into acute myelogenous leukemia. Dr. William "Nick" Nichols quietly observed that his new patient now shared the same disease that had killed her dear friend. Dr. Nichols could only hope that the optimism and fighting spirit exuded by both friends would lead to a better conclusion for Sandy.

With no time to lose, Sandy immediately began chemotherapy to arrest the raging blood disease. Whenever she needed chemotherapy or other treatment, the Sargents rented the Montana Cancer Center's one-bedroom apartment, augmenting the usual furnishings with "office" furniture—identical white plastic lawn chairs and two card tables, one blue and one green.

For the Sargent family, life in Missoula presented a new routine. Son Rick would join his parents for three to four weeks at a time and daughter Kerri would fly from her home in Issaquah, Washington, whenever she could leave her own children. The loving support of Rick and Kerri, combined with Len's constant presence, reassured Sandy as she received life-giving blood and chemotherapy in the cancer center's treatment room. Still, tethered to an IV pole and chain-reading mystery thrillers, Sandy fretted whenever Len's daily walk led him away from her to chocolate milkshake therapy at his favorite riverfront ice cream shop. She worried constantly about the effects of Len's sweet tooth on his high blood pressure and high cholesterol levels, but acknowledged that at least the walk did him some good.

Whenever Sandy was able, the Sargents met friends for dinner or attended local meetings and political events. In longhand or typing on her first computer, Sandy wrote about their altered lives, showing mild irritation when her disease interfered with their plans, celebrating the chemically induced remissions she experienced, and profusely thanking Rick and Judi, Kerri, and the Sargents' many friends for their presence and support. Even while fighting the battle of her life, Sandy never forgot her manners, apologizing in one mass mailing "to the many visitors I had to miss seeing and to those whose meetings we had to forego."

In March 1996, Sandy's longest remission allowed the Sargents to make a second trip through the Panama Canal Zone, where they resumed their search for the street named after Len's father. While "Canal transits were fascinating" and the Sargents basked in the "royal spoiling" by the crew, they never located Leonard R. Sargent Street, Sandy lamented in a postcard to my family. Typically, though, they ran into "one of Len's former students (whose father he also taught!)," and got a special tour of the Smithsonian Tropical Research Institution on an island off the coast of Panama. And typically, Sandy closed with, "You've all been so in our thoughts....Many hugs & much love. S&L." A postcard or letter from Sandy was a metaphor for her life, filled to the edges with enthusiasm, energy, passion, and love.

As they split their time between Missoula and their homes in Santa Barbara and Bozeman, the Sargents tried to keep their lives as "normal" as possible. They stayed involved with "numerous environmental groups," but they could not ignore the elephant in the room. Sandy's cancer made both of them worry about what would happen to the other if the worst scenario came to pass. Sandy often confided that she did not know how Len would cope without her constant attention to detail if she were not around to help him.

Len openly expressed his concerns about Sandy's health to both family and friends and enlisted their support in urging her to slow down. Len even asked several of their Valle Verde friends to help him plead the case for wintering in Santa Barbara, where the couple could offer their talents to a local environmental fund-raising effort instead of traveling, as planned, to the Seychelles, a group of islands off the east coast of Africa. Dr. Nichols had warned against the trip the Sargents had scheduled for early 1997, but Sandy was determined.

In December 1996, Len discussed his worries with a longtime Montana friend, Susan Cottingham. Would Sandy have enough strength for a vacation halfway around the world, let alone for all those Christmas cards with the newsy, typed message and handwritten personal notes? Len knew how much their family and friends looked forward to those annual holiday missives, but would they understand if Sandy skipped a year?

Back in Santa Barbara, the Sargents' debate over the trip to the Seychelles was pre-empted when Len collapsed on his daily walk and needed hospitalization for a blood clot in the leg, one his doctor feared could move to his heart. Sandy was furious that Len's health, not hers, might keep them from visiting the Seychelles. Depleted and exhausted, Len was relieved when daughter-in-law Judi Stauffer calmed Sandy by agreeing to take his spot on the trip. A few days after Len's release from the hospital, Sandy misjudged a curb, fell, and broke her arm. No one was going to the Seychelles.

Nevertheless, 400 holiday letters hit the mail on schedule, same as always.

In early February 1997, Sandy relapsed, and she, Len, and Rick returned to Missoula. One day, while Sandy was leashed to chemotherapy, Len took his daily stroll around downtown Missoula and "to his surprise he inadvertently wandered into a rally," Jim Posewitz later told mourners at Len's memorial service. "Upon learning the rally was a protest over the inexcusable treatment of bison, [Len] joined the march," Posewitz continued. "The sheer joy of it lifted his spirits. Unaware that the sand in his hourglass had about run out, [Len] was literally running in the streets for the principles he cherished. He deeply treasured the exhilaration of the moment."

A few days after the bison protest, Len and I walked and talked our way around Missoula's North Side. Fully recovered from the blood clot scare, Len appeared healthy but concerned enough about his blood pressure to choose a route that avoided his favorite ice cream parlor and the temptation to feed his chocolate addiction. He told me, not for the first time, that he worried constantly about Sandy's precarious health as she continued to try to maximize every hour of every day.

Another round of chemotherapy complete, the Sargents left Missoula and returned to their condominium in Bozeman to resume their "normal" life, and Rick returned home to California. Soon after all had settled in, on February 16, 1997, the Sargents were scheduled to attend a morning coffee for Democratic presidential candidate Bill Bradley, but Len felt queasy and urged Sandy to attend for them both. She did, but when she returned home, Len was feeling much worse, so she called an ambulance.

As Sandy filled out the paperwork in the emergency room of Bozeman Deaconess Hospital, Len died much as he had lived, quietly and without a lot of fuss.

Meanwhile, 1,300 miles away, Rick and Judi were backpacking in the San Raphael Wilderness near their Santa Barbara home, celebrating both Rick's birthday and Valentine's Day. Spending summers and holidays in Cinnabar Basin had taught them about the healing powers of wild solitude. Now Rick sought the wilderness to help smooth the roller coaster of emotions he had experienced throughout the two tumultuous years of his mother's illness. On February 16, several days into their hike, Rick awoke with a chilling premonition, and he knew he had to head home. Hastily loading his backpack, Rick set off down the trail.

"As I was walking in the door that evening, my sister called and said, 'Dad died this afternoon.' " The next day, Rick flew to his mother's side in Montana.

Although Len was 84 years old, his fatal heart attack surprised almost everyone the Sargents knew. Friends and family had assumed Sandy would die first because of her disease. Sandy did, too, and had given several of us an extensive list of family and friends with telephone numbers and addresses. "Mainly to help Len's sometimes forgetfulness (!), but please file in case you can help R&K [Rick and Kerri] one day," she noted.

Sandy reacted to Len's death characteristically. She hit the "get organized" button and planned every conceivable detail of the memorial service for her popular and well-known husband—reserving hotel rooms for out-of-town guests; delicately scheduling an Episcopal memorial service in the more spacious Presbyterian Church; planning seating arrangements for family and close friends; arranging a post-service reception in Bozeman's historic Baxter Hotel; and, finally, delegating responsibility for program-writing and for shuttling out-of-towners—all the while graciously greeting each visitor who stopped by the condo.

Everything came off just as Sandy had planned. Len's memorial service was standing room only. Family, friends, activists, politicians, and former caretakers attended from all over the country. Speakers praised Len for his profound environmental ethic, his bottomless generosity, and his humanity. The congregation celebrated Len's life with "For the Beauty of the Earth" and "For All the Saints." As mourners filed out, they pinned on buttons sporting Len's image, symbols of remembrance and community similar to the "PT" buttons worn by many of the same people when Phil Tawney died.

Grief did not dim Sandy's conservation fervor or her eagerness to give advice. Recently retired after 18 years in Congress, Pat Williams waited patiently to speak to her after the lengthy church service, a reversal of roles from that wilderness hearing so many years before. "I hung around," he recalled. "When she saw me, she came over and kissed me on the cheek. She took my hand and she held it, and she said, 'Pat, you do what you know is right. Don't compromise just to be compromising.' She knew I wasn't in Congress anymore. Her point was about the future. Stick to your guns. 'Len would want me to tell you this.' "

A few days after the memorial service, in a move reminiscent of her husband's just weeks earlier, Sandy joined a gang of young protestors picketing Bozeman's federal building, trying (successfully, it turned out) to stop the Forest Service from moving ahead with an ill-conceived timber sale in the Hyalite Basin.

"An unsuspecting TV reporter approached her and asked her to comment," Jim Jensen wrote in the August 1997 issue of MEIC's newsletter, *Down to Earth*. "Her response was swift, passionate and persuasive. The reporter was visibly impressed (and surprised)."

Sandy spent the next few months in motion. She stayed in Bozeman whenever she could but set up housekeeping in Missoula whenever she needed chemotherapy. Montana became Rick's temporary home once again as he accompanied his mother to her treatments and shared her Missoula apartment. Rick's wife Judi joined them when she could steal time away from her job, adding her grace and perspective to the family crisis. Kerri periodically came to Missoula to relieve Rick when she could break away from her own responsibilities as the mother of three active girls.

In March, after completing another round of chemotherapy, Sandy flew alone to Santa Barbara and spent several weeks at Rick and Judi's home in the Santa Ynez Valley and at her own home in Valle Verde. From Santa Barbara, Sandy launched, in retrospect, a goodbye tour, wrapping up the loose ends of her remarkable life before joining Leonard in death. She traveled to Rye and Bronxville, New York, to visit relatives and friends; to Connecticut and her alma mater Westover School where she toured a garden established in honor of her sister Debby, who had died in a car accident a year earlier. Then, Sandy was off to The Taft School for a memorial service honoring alumni and faculty, including Len, who had died within the last year; and to New York City for an organ concert at the Cathedral of St. John the Divine, where she had attended a service for the Blessing of the Animals a few years earlier.

By early June, Sandy's medical condition had taken a drastic turn for the worse, but before returning to Montana for more medical treatments, she accompanied Judi to a fund-raising dinner with the XVI Dalai Lama. The dinner was part of a campaign to raise money for a new chair in religious studies established in the Dalai Lama's name at the University of California-Santa Barbara.

On July 5, the pastor of the Bronxville Reformed Church, where Sandy had worked as a young divorced mother, eulogized Leonard and honored Sandy for their lives of active commitment. In his sermon that day, the Reverend Richard Lichti told the congregation, "Leonard Sargent was a man of tender conscience." Then the pastor praised the Sargent legacy:

...Together Len and Sandy possessed an unselfish passion to bring people together and focus their energies constructively on taking better care of the environment.

Not ones to stand by on the sidelines, Len and Sandy believed in the importance of not judging other people too quickly. They taught fellow environmentalists not to see things only as "us versus them."

Len and Sandy were known for their powerful witness in the midst of contentious hearings: holding their ground, speaking lovingly and eloquently.

Realizing in the 1970s that resource exploiters were wining and dining the legislators of the Montana legislature, Len and Sandy founded and funded a party at the beginning of each session.

For the last 20 years that bipartisan gathering has been the highlight of the legislature's social calendar.

Len and Sandy well knew the brokenness of the political process, but they never underestimated its redemptive possibilities.

And so, the tender conscience is energized not by what we possess, or do not possess, but by that which is promised.

Though they often fussed at each other—Sandy more than Len—the Sargents finished each other's sentences and brought complementary talents to their marriage of nearly 28 years. More reserved and diplomatic, Len was the couple's public spokesman. A high-energy multitasker, Sandy took copious notes, helped frame arguments, and cheered on Len.

Len's unexpected death had caught Sandy off-guard. She was not prepared to survive her husband and losing him clearly diminished her spirit. After the hubbub surrounding his memorial service, the heady picketing that followed, and her sentimental journey East, Sandy lost much of her old fight and her leukemia resumed its attack on her bloodstream. For five months after Len's death, Sandy publicly kept up a strong and smiling front, but inside she must have been imploding. The Sargents' Montana friends all underestimated the power of Sandy's love for and her dependence upon Len.

She spent her final days in a coma, unconscious, her body unmoving on the hospital bed, but within her remained a spark, the ability to respond to good news from a dear friend.

Phil Tawney and Sandy had shared more than boundless energy, a love of networking, and a deep commitment to the environment: They shared the same variety of cancer and now Sandy was dying, too. My late husband and I had been married just a day after the Sargents in 1969. When he died at age 45, Phil Tawney was regarded as one of Montana's most influential conservationists and his death hit the green community hard, especially the Sargents, who had loved and treated him like a son.

Yet, when I began dating again, nobody was happier for me than Len and Sandy, especially since I was seeing Dr. Nick Nichols, the man who had tended my late husband and became Sandy's oncologist, too. When Nick and I announced our engagement, the Sargents were ecstatic. Given the circumstances of Sandy's illness, she was gladly forgiven for nagging us about setting a wedding date. Clearly, she wanted to be there for the big day.

By the time we finally picked our day, Len was gone and Sandy was hovering near death. Still, I wanted Sandy to be among the first to know, so I gently took her hand. In response to my happy news, Sandy squeezed my hand. Through her coma, she squeezed my hand.

Sandy died a few days later, on July 22, 1997, her children at her side, as she had been at her own mother's deathbed four years earlier. Sandy's mother lived to be 96 years young; Sandy was just 75.

As Sandy had requested, her memorial service on September 29, 1997, so soon after Len's, was a smaller and lower key affair held in Bozeman's century-old St. James Episcopal Church. This time, the mourners were fewer and the post-service reception was held in the church fellowship hall.

Sandy's understated service included some of the elements of Len's memorial: the hymn "For All the Saints," tributes by Sandy's children Rick and Kerri, and the Sargents' friend Jim Posewitz. Where friends of the only child had completed the sketch of Len's life, Sandy's remaining sisters and a couple of old friends filled in hers.

"None of us shall ever forget Sandy Sargent," Posewitz wrote, "the woman who brought fire to our cause, elegance into our presence, and a lot of class to every cause she championed. She was the irrepressible full participant. When she joined an organization or chose a battle, she came in full measure and there was no one more reliable or more durable."

He called Sandy, "the champion of our possibility." Nothing could be more true.

Leaving a legacy

A few days after Sandy's memorial service, Bruce Gordon, a pilot for Project Lighthawk, flew Rick, Kerri, Judi, and Sandy's surviving sisters Karen DePlanque and Sabra Cleveland above Cinnabar Basin to scatter the Sargents' ashes over their former ranch. For Len and Sandy, a long chapter had ended, but their story was not over.

Because the Sargents took seriously their responsibilities as citizens of Montana and the greater Yellowstone area, they influenced others of greater and lesser means to do likewise. Through advocacy, mentoring, inclusiveness, and timely donations, Len and Sandy made a difference. And by designating significant gifts from the bulk of their considerable estate, they made sure that their financial resources would continue to support the work they had helped start for a long time to come.

Eighty percent of the Sargents' assets endowed the Cinnabar Foundation and environmental organizations that serve Montana and the greater Yellowstone area. Ironically, these bequests—while certainly welcomed and appreciated—ran a distant second to the Sargents' earlier life-giving contributions of time and money. By 1997, the groups Len and Sandy had nurtured from their beginnings, including the Montana Environmental Information Center and the Greater Yellowstone Coalition, were long-established, credible, and professional nonprofits. While the Sargents' generous bequests certainly helped, the recipient groups were in no danger of imploding, as they had been 20 years earlier.

As activists and philanthropists, the Sargents saw environmentalism become a mainstream movement and environmental groups become active and respected participants in the political, economic, and natural landscapes of Montana and the greater Yellowstone area. While those organizations might have persisted without the Sargents' support, Len and Sandy certainly helped accelerate their growth and their power, and helped them grow roots deep and wide.

"These people did not complain," recalled their accountant, Ernest Turner. "They did not expect. They acted. They worked and they gave."

For much of their lives, the Sargents did the majority of their work quietly and behind the scenes—leading from behind—and they enjoyed every minute of it. They did all they could to help build strong organizations, but to Len, the time and money spent were never enough. Each year, when the Cinnabar Foundation board met to decide how to allocate available funds, Len always would lament, "I wish I could've given more."

That is a statement worth pondering.

Today the Sargent legacy lives directly and indirectly through the groups they funded, the people they nurtured, and the work those people went on to do. It lives on in the endowments of the Greater Yellowstone Coalition and the Montana Environmental Information Center, so munificently augmented by Sargent bequests. It lives on through the Len and Sandy Sargent Chair in Western Lands, a senior staff position permanently endowed by Len's bequest to the Natural Resources Defense Council. And it lives on through the Cinnabar Foundation, which Len and Sandy lovingly created as a perpetual source of funding and support for groups on the frontlines of the environmental movement in Montana and the greater Yellowstone area.

None of this would have happened if Len and Sandy had not planned for it. Early in their marriage, they recognized how financial woes distracted nonprofit organizations from their missions and decided to provide ongoing support through planned giving. Len and Sandy made careful and thoughtful choices about their financial resources and made sure they clearly designated those choices in their wills. Their foresight is a lesson to us all.

Careful planning by "true believers" like the Sargents can sustain our wildlife and wild lands far into the future. As long as these natural resources remain the target of misuse and development by those who seek a quick buck without consequences, organizations that address the tough issues will need adequate funding. As long as government support—at every level— continues to shrink and the private sector is called upon to pick up the slack, our help is needed. The issues facing our natural resources may change over time, but they will not go away, and it behooves all of us to participate in the perpetual work of advocacy, research, and education.

Although we may regularly volunteer or donate to nonprofits, such support will be sorely missed when we are gone unless we, like Len and

Sandy, designate specific gifts in our wills. A financial adviser can explain the benefits of making bequests through wills, trusts, or other legal vehicles. Bequests of any size are welcomed and signal our wish to see the good work of charitable organizations continued in perpetuity.

Through their long years of activism and perpetual philanthropy, the Sargents left a fine legacy. We can do the same.

After a while, Len said, and I realized later he was probably reaching back to some moment in his own life, "How lucky you are. How lucky you are to have had a night when you were so full of ideas and exhilaration that you couldn't sleep."

...in that spirit and on behalf of Len and Sandy...trust your idealism, trust the ideas clanging against all the walls of your minds, trust them as your most precious tangible possessions, and trust them now, for this is your moment.

— Charles Wilkinson, from his keynote address at the 1993 Cinnabar Foundation Symposium, *Endangered Species in Timber Country*

Zeke, leading from behind.
Drawing by Jim Stevens

Select Bibliography

Alt, David, and Donald Hyndman. *Roadside Geology of Montana.* Missoula, Mont.: Mountain Press Publishing Company, 1986.

Barker, Rocky. "Grassroots grit beat 'the mine from Hell.'" *High Country News,* Vol. 28, No. 16, September 2, 1996.

Benedetto, Kathleen. *Testimony on the American Land Sovereignty Protection Act, S510.* Presented to Subcommittee on Forests and Public Land Management of the Senate Committee on Energy and Natural Resources, 106th Cong., 1999.

Cunningham, Bill. *Montana Wildlands.* Number 16 of *Montana Geographic Series.* Helena, Mont.: American Geographic Publishing, 1990.

Donat, Hank. "The San Franciscans: Barnaby Conrad III." www.mistersf.com/sanfran/sanfranbarnaby.htm, 2001.

Greater Yellowstone Coalition. *Annual Report.* Bozeman, Mont.: Greater Yellowstone Coalition, 2002.

Jacobs, Mike. *One Time Harvest.* Jamestown, N.D.: Farmers Union, 1975.

Jensen, Jim. "Thoughts from the Executive Director." *Down to Earth.* Helena, Mont.: Montana Environmental Information Center, August 1997.

"Leonard Rundlett Sargent, Jr." *Missoulian (Missoula, Mont.),* n.d., 1997.

Lichti, Rev. Dr. Richard. "Sermon." Bronxville, N.Y., July 5, 1997.

McMillion, Scott. "Len and Sandy Sargent." *We Montanans,* Supplement to *Montana Magazine,* 1994, 20-21.

Ibid. "Noted environmentalist dies at 84." *Bozeman (Montana) Daily Chronicle,* n.d, 1997.

"Merriam 'Sandy' Sands Packard Sargent." *Review Press-Reporter (Bronxville, N.Y.),* July 31, 1997.

Montaigne, Fen. "A gold mine in Montana is a lode of controversy." *The Philadelphia Inquirer,* n.d., 1995.

Montana Environmental Information Center. *20th Anniversary Report: 1974-1994.* Helena, Mont.: Montana Environmental Information Center, 1994.

Montana Department of Fish, Wildlife & and Parks. *A Century of Conservation,* Special Centennial Issue of *Montana Outdoors,* November/December 2000.

Odden, Lance R. "Leonard Sargent." *Taft Bulletin,* Spring 1997, 11-13.

Pierce, Kevin. "Restoring the Kissimmee River." Radio Program by www.FloridaEnvironment.com, July 31, 2000.

Posewitz, James. "Leonard Sargent Eulogy: Sarge." Bozeman, Mont., February 21, 1997.

Ibid. "Merriam Sands Packard Sargent: Sandy." Bozeman, Mont., September 29, 1997.

Ibid. "Preserving Paradise." In *Montana's Yellowstone River.*
   Number 10 of *Montana Geographic Series.* Helena, Mont.: Montana
   Magazine, Inc., 1985.

Ibid. "The Sleeping Giant." In *Montana's Yellowstone River.*
   Number 10 of *Montana Geographic Series.* Helena, Mont.: Montana
   Magazine, Inc., 1985.

Reid, Allis Beaumont. Letter to William Nichols, August 6, 1997.

Sargent, Leonard, and Sandy Sargent. Audiotaped interview by Susan Neel,
   October 6, 1995.

Ibid. Holiday letters, 1976-1995.

Ibid. Letters to Robin Tawney, 1976-1997.

Ibid. Letters to Robin and Phil Tawney, 1976-1995.

Ibid. Letters to Robin Tawney and William Nichols, 1996-1997.

Ibid. Telephone interview by Robin Tawney, January 3, n.d.

Ibid. Videotaped interview by Gayle Joslin, 1994.

Schneider, Bill. *Montana's Yellowstone River.* Number 10 of *Montana
   Geographic Series.* Helena, Mont.: Montana Magazine, Inc., 1985.

Spritzer, Don. *Roadside History of Montana.* Missoula, Mont.: Mountain
   Press Publishing Company, 1999.

Staley, Oliver. "Longtime conservation activist dies in Missoula." *Bozeman
   Daily Chronicle,* July 25, 1997.

Tawney, Robin. *Family Fun in Yellowstone National Park.* Guildford, Conn.:
   The Globe Pequot Press, 2001.

Ibid. "Len and Sandy Sargent." *Montana Magazine,* n.d.

Ibid. "Strip Mining: Clarifying the Issue." *UM Profiles,* Vol. 5, No. 2,
   November 1972, 4-5.

Tawney, Robin, and Phil Tawney. *EIC: Building a Citizens Organization to
   Last. The NRAG Papers,* Vol. 2, No. 3, Winter 1977-78.

Toole, K. Ross. *The Rape of the Great Plains.* Boston: Little, Brown and
   Company, 1976.

Woodwell, Caroline. "Sargents' Gift Creates GYC Endowment." *Greater
   Yellowstone Coalition Report,* Fall 1997, 20.

About the Author

Robin Tawney Nichols lives in a forested canyon on the outskirts of Missoula, Montana, with her husband William Nichols, two dogs, one cat, two horses, and an occasional pet spider.

Committed to conservation stewardship and education, Robin serves on the boards of the Cinnabar Foundation and the Philip D. Tawney Hunters Conservation Endowment of the Montana Wildlife Federation. Robin and her late husband Phil Tawney shared recognition for their conservation work as recipients of a 1976 Chevron Conservation Award and as the 1995 Conservationist of the Year, an award given by the Montana Environmental Information Center. In 2000, the Missoula Conservation Roundtable honored Robin as Conservationist of the Year.

A journalism graduate of the University of Montana, Robin also is the author of Hiking with Kids (Falcon Publishing, 2000 and 2007, *Family Fun in Yellowstone* (Falcon Publishing, 1998), and *Young People's Guide to Yellowstone National Park* (Stoneydale Press, 1985). Robin's byline has appeared in state, regional, and national newspapers and magazines.